OVERWHELMED BY CONSTANT MENTAL CHATTER? TRIED EVERYTHING TO QUIET YOUR MIND BUT NOTHING WORKS?

Overthink offers innovative strategies to help you silence mental noise and regain control of your thoughts. Instead of shutting them down, you'll learn to think in a way that truly serves you. Drawing on a decade of research and insights from hundreds of overthinkers, this practical guide explains why common advice often falls short and provides a smarter approach to calm, effective thinking.

With relatable examples and hands-on techniques, *Overthink* delivers valuable insights on every page, including:

- How your thoughts and unconscious mind work
- The unproductive thoughts that keep you stuck
- A simple three-step method to reclaim your mind
- Ways to build confidence and a growth mindset
- Practical strategies to increase your success

This isn't just about silencing your thoughts. It's about transforming them into a powerful tool for clarity, confidence, and purposeful action. *Overthink* isn't just a book; it's a roadmap to a calmer, sharper, and more empowered mind.

WHAT READERS ARE SAYING ABOUT
Overthink

"I finally found a tool to manage my constant stream of thoughts." —Yuliia

"Wonderful book with great nuggets to stop the chatter and, more importantly, improve your thoughts." —D.N.

"This book is a goldmine." —F.F.

"Eye-opening and gave me real tools to think clearly without feeling overwhelmed." —Sam F.

"Packed with useful new information I hadn't come across before." —Analogica

"It's a refreshing, straightforward approach to help you regain control over your thoughts, without overcomplicating the process." —Lauren P.

"A Must-Read Book!" —Z.N.

"A concise and approachable look at managing overthinking and anxiety." —Erin A.

"A surprisingly genuine and honest read that cuts through a lot of the noise that surrounds this genre." —Vince

"With Overthink, you can take control of your thoughts and create a healthier, happier mindset." —Midwest Book Review

"Filled with innovative and invaluable insights. This book has the potential to spark significant introspection and growth." —International Review of Books

THOUGHTBOOKS

Middle Think

Clear Think

Big Think

overthink

/noun/

a sign that your thoughts are unproductive, and an opportunity to shift toward more effective thinking.

OVERTHINK

OVERTHINK

CALM THOUGHTS

LYNDSEY GETTY

THE THOUGHT METHOD CO.

To anyone who has ever replayed a conversation on repeat

CONTENTS

INTRODUCTION

Nearly everyone struggles with the repetitive thoughts and irritating mental chatter of overthinking. It's a common frustration affecting 73 percent of people aged 25–35 and 52 percent of those aged 45–55.[1] To put it simply, if you catch yourself replaying social interactions after a party, chances are that most of the other attendees are doing the same thing.

Traditional advice suggests that overthinking is merely thinking "too much," and the solution is for us to somehow reduce our thoughts. But this approach sets us up for failure. Mindfulness techniques and attempts to quiet the mental noise might offer temporary relief, but they only scratch the surface.

To stop the mental chatter and eliminate unwanted and repetitive thoughts for good, we need to dig deeper. We need to identify and address the unproductive thoughts that are leading us into the spiral. Because what's commonly labeled as "overthinking" is actually *unproduc-*

tive thinking. And the goal isn't to stop our thoughts, it's to make them more productive.

Productive thinking is when you manage your thoughts to support your mental well-being and align with your values and goals. When thoughts are productive, you naturally opt for quality over quantity, eliminating the tendency to "overthink" or judge your thoughts on the disastrously unproductive over/under scale.

Making this seemingly simple shift will have a significant impact. Your mind doesn't register "don'ts," so if someone tells you, "Don't think of a red balloon," you will likely imagine a red balloon. In all likelihood, you're picturing one right now because I mentioned it. And if I ask you to deliberately *stop* thinking about a red balloon, your thoughts may be overrun with red balloons. The more you think about how you *don't* want to think about red balloons, the more you think about those darn red balloons. This is similar to when you think about how you want to stop thinking so much and end up thinking more. If you are reading this book, I am sure you can relate.

Being productive in your thinking involves under-standing this psychological quirk and actively choosing to focus on what you want, rather than what you don't. When it comes to "overthinking," instead of trying to stop the incessant thoughts, which will intensify the mental chatter and frustration, shifting your focus to what you want, to think more productively, will reduce the mental noise. So, rather than saying, "I want to stop thinking as much," you'd say, "I am going to make my thoughts work for me."

Ideally, we would have been taught how to think productively in childhood, but traditional education does not put much emphasis in this area. So here you will get a welcome and overdue crash course on how thoughts work and how to make your thoughts productive. These concepts can be tricky so I'll break them down with just enough detail to provide a practical yet effective understanding. In my experience, this is all the average person needs to know so they can create healthier, more productive thoughts.

But before moving forward, it is important to acknowledge how far you've already come. Realizing you are "overthinking" is you becoming aware of your unproductive thoughts. Self-awareness is an incredible skill that, when cultivated, has the power to change your life. While annoying, those repetitive thoughts are forcing you out of your comfort zone so you can build your awareness and come into your true potential. Cheers to you!

ARE YOUR THOUGHTS PRODUCTIVE?

You have a wedgie but there's an attractive person in eyesight. Do you pick it? What should you have for dinner? They haven't replied to your text. How long ago did you send it? Should you send a follow-up or would that seem too eager? Are you coming off as clingy again? What now? You just remembered that cringey thing you did in grade school. Oh great, you just remembered that embarrassing thing you did last week.

In this complicated and chaotic world, there's a lot to think about. Since we haven't been taught how to think productively, we often make it more complicated and chaotic than it needs to be.

Unproductive thoughts look like:

- going over the same things repeatedly, even when you try to stop
- continually doubting your abilities and decisions
- replaying past events, examining every detail
- excessively thinking about anxiety-inducing or scary situations
- being hard on yourself and questioning if you're good enough
- expecting worst-case scenarios, even when they're unlikely
- struggling to move past mistakes or missed opportunities
- worrying about what other people might think
- striving for perfection while fearing failure
- feeling overwhelmed with racing thoughts
- feeling ashamed about past events or thoughts you've had

SELF-ASSESSMENT

This quiz will help you figure out if your thoughts are unproductive. Check all that apply.

In social situations, you...

❏ replay interactions in your mind, analyzing every detail

❏ worry a lot about how others perceive you

❏ frequently second-guess the things you say or do

❏ avoid certain social events because you fear making mistakes or feeling out of place

❏ find it hard to start or maintain conversations because you're afraid of saying the wrong thing

❏ feel anxious or self-conscious before, during, or after social gatherings

❏ obsessively plan and rehearse what to say or how to act in social situations

❏ often feel like you don't fit in or belong

❏ dwell on embarrassing moments long after they've occurred

❏ believe others are constantly looking at you or judging you, even when there's no evidence to support it

____ checked

With self-care and daily routines, you...

❏ struggle to relax because your mind is always busy with thoughts

❏ frequently feel guilty when you take time for self-care, thinking you should be doing something more "productive"

❏ overanalyze your daily routines and habits, trying to optimize every aspect of your life

❏ feel overwhelmed by your to-do list and have difficulty deciding what to prioritize
❏ worry excessively about minor decisions like what to wear or eat
❏ frequently compare yourself to others and feel like you're not good enough
❏ have difficulty saying no to requests or commitments even when you're already stretched thin
❏ constantly think about work or responsibilities even during leisure time
❏ often procrastinate on important tasks because you're stuck in thought
❏ find it challenging to disconnect from technology and be fully in the moment
____ checked

When thinking about the future, you...
❏ spend a lot of time worrying about what will or might happen
❏ have trouble making decisions because you're afraid of making the wrong choice
❏ obsessively plan and prepare, often expecting worst-case scenarios
❏ frequently feel anxious or stressed about the uncertainty of the future
❏ set impossibly high standards for future goals and feel overwhelmed by the pressure to achieve them
❏ are so focused on reaching your future goals that you forget to enjoy the journey

❏ get so caught up in worries you find it difficult to enjoy the present moment

❏ find it challenging to trust that things will work out without excessive planning

❏ worry about future regrets or missed opportunities

❏ frequently ask others for reassurance about your future decisions or plans

____ checked

After making mistakes, you...

❏ often dwell on past mistakes or regrets, making it hard to let them go

❏ replay scenarios in your head, thinking about how things could have gone differently

❏ feel embarrassed or ashamed about past errors, even if they were minor

❏ have difficulty forgiving yourself for past mistakes or perceived failures

❏ think other people judge you for your past mistakes, even if they don't know about them

❏ avoid taking risks or trying new things because you fear making mistakes

❏ dwell on past criticism or negative feedback, even if it was constructive

❏ frequently feel the need to explain or justify your past actions to others

❏ have difficulty accepting that making mistakes is a natural part of life

❏ carry past mistakes with you that impact your self-esteem and confidence

_____ checked

If you've experienced trauma, you...
❏ keep thinking about how you could have avoided the traumatic event
❏ wonder if seeking help is worth the risk of not being believed
❏ constantly replay the traumatic event in your mind and feel overwhelmed by its lasting impact
❏ experience intrusive thoughts related to a traumatic event
❏ have recurring nightmares or distressing dreams related to past trauma
_____ checked

TOTAL CHECKED: _____ out of 45

Many of us deal with racing thoughts and mental chatter from time to time, but if you checked fifteen or more boxes, it's likely your thoughts are unproductive. The difference is that people with unproductive thinking *often* deal with excessive mental chatter and racing thoughts, making life harder than it needs to be and leading to both mental and physical health issues.

For example, if you're tired after socializing because you keep analyzing everything you said and did, you might start avoiding social situations altogether. This can lead to loneliness, strain relationships, and cause or heighten social anxiety.

If your mind is constantly filled with mental noise, you'll likely have trouble concentrating, feel stuck, and give up on goals. You'll not only feel mentally exhausted but also less happy and confident.

Unproductive thinkers often struggle to enjoy the present moment, falling into cycles of worrying about the past or future. This ongoing worry can lead to restlessness, difficulty sleeping, and anxiety-related symptoms, like headaches and tense muscles. The physical symptoms make it hard to stay active, intensifying unproductive thoughts, since physical activity helps clear the mind. This self-perpetuating cycle is demotivating and leaves even the most driven individuals feeling hopeless. Breaking free from this pattern is crucial for reclaiming mental well-being and building a more satisfying life.

WHO THIS BOOK IS FOR

This book is not just about identifying unproductive thoughts; it's a guide to transforming your mental landscape and reclaiming control over your life. While directed toward those struggling with repetitive and unwanted thoughts, it is equally valuable for anyone seeking to improve their mindset and make lasting and positive change.

Even though "overthinking" isn't considered a mental illness, it can worsen depression and anxiety, and is linked to c-PTSD (complex PTSD) and PTSD.[2] Mastering the skill of nurturing productive thoughts not only equips you with the tools to combat "overthinking" but also unlocks the potential for a more fulfilling and resilient mindset.

THE STATS

To understand why people tend to "overthink," and pinpoint the most common types of unproductive thoughts that lead to mental chatter, I went to the source and asked "overthinkers" *why* they overthink. To keep it authentic, I collected insights in a relaxed format using social media for its original purpose: connection. A simple prompt was posted in different forums on multiple social media sites: "I'm working on a book about overcoming overthinking. If you're prone to overthink, would you share what you overthink about?"

From there, I used my experience of over a decade in tech operations to aggregate the responses from more than 300 overthinkers and get what we call in the industry, "strategic insights." Responses were first put into two main categories: overthinking and rumination. Though these terms are often used interchangeably, "overthinking" involves fixating on the future while "rumination" centers around dwelling on the past (both signify unproductive thoughts).

Interestingly, 83 percent of respondents reported thinking about the future, while only 17 percent ruminated on the past. Responses were then separated into five common triggers.

TRIGGERS	OVER-THINKING	RUMI-NATION
Social Interactions	40%	60%
Day-to-Day Planning	31%	—
Future Planning	29%	—
Perceived Mistakes	—	24%
Trauma	—	8%
Philosophical Pondering	—	8%

Social interactions, such as replaying past conversations, worrying about other people's opinions, being mindful not to offend anyone, setting up appointments, dating, and interacting with coworkers, were the most common things people repeatedly thought about. Next came everyday concerns like deciding what to have for dinner, whether to make an expensive purchase, and handling new parenting challenges. Lastly, planning for the future, considering a career change, furthering education, organizing a vacation, and buying presents were the third most common things people shared.

About a quarter of rumination involved dwelling on mistakes, such as saying or doing something silly or buying something just before it went on sale. Reflecting on past experiences, such as feeling manipulated, traumatic events like car accidents, and contemplating deeper aspects of life, such as wondering why people do the things they do, each accounted for about 8 percent of the time spent ruminating.

THE INSIGHTS

Concepts commonly associated with "overthinking," such as fear, control, and perfectionism, were present in most responses. However, all responses indicated either a fixed mindset, unhelpful thinking habits known as "cognitive distortions," or low self-confidence. Many of them displayed two or more of these elements.

For example, if you often worry about whether you should pursue a goal or if you'll succeed, it's probably due to a lack of confidence and a cognitive distortion called "should thinking."

If you excessively dwell on every social interaction regardless of its importance, it likely comes from having a fixed mindset and low self-confidence.

And if you believe that you can never move past a mistake you made, it's likely due to a fixed mindset and the cognitive distortion known as "all-or-nothing" thinking.

These concepts, which we'll call "root causes," suggest that fixed mindsets, unhelpful thinking habits, and low self-confidence are the main reasons for repetitive and unproductive thoughts. By creating a growth mindset, emphasizing balanced thinking, and boosting your confidence, you will develop productive thought habits and eliminate excessive thoughts altogether.

HOW I FOUND THE "OVERTHINKING" CURE

Identifying the root causes made me realize something I hadn't noticed before. I was already, unknowingly, working on the root causes, but I didn't realize that building a growth mindset, correcting cognitive distortions, and increasing my confidence were helping me stop my excessive, and seemingly never-ending, thoughts. In fact, when I first started focusing on my mental health, it wasn't about managing thoughts; it was to make sure I didn't end up in jail.

My story is like many others who don't realize they have depression, c-PTSD, or anxiety that controls their lives. I slept a lot, thought it was cool to hate everyone, worked and drank too much. This was my normal so seeking help didn't even cross my mind. I was in my "comfort zone" and had no idea I was a miserable workaholic, people-pleasing perfectionist with no boundaries, crippling social anxiety, and low confidence who drank her feelings.

Then came the anger. It was intense and I couldn't seem to shake it. Scared I might lose my cool and end up in trouble, I would watch prison-related TV shows as an odd reminder not to do something dumb. People who know me find it hard to believe the woman who sometimes sounds like *Schitt's Creek*'s Alexis Rose could be so angry. I am naturally a silly (and sometimes annoyingly happy) person, so reaching this point truly highlighted how far I was from myself.

In an attempt to return to me, I tried things like exercise, yoga, and journaling. They helped a bit, but I was still that angry, people-pleasing perfectionist who worked, drank, and worried too much—now just with smaller-size jeans (from all the exercise) and prettier penmanship (from all the journaling).

Out of sheer desperation, I went to therapy. Growing up I was taught that therapy was for losers who want to blame their parents, so I felt like a coward. Finding the right therapist was tough. I walked out on one mid-session. Others didn't think they could help me, labeling me one of the worst cases of childhood abuse they had ever seen.

Then I finally caught a break, a child therapist who specializes in cognitive behavioral therapy (CBT). At work I was managing and negotiating millions of dollars' worth of contracts and talking with CEOs and executive leadership. Then I would drive to my new therapist's office and sit in the colorful waiting room with toys and dollhouses for the pediatric patients.

While I was grateful to have one hour a week to talk about my feelings, and my new therapist was helping me, it felt painfully slow and not enough to make the significant impact I needed. Seeing my frustration, my therapist recommended a book that completely changed how I approached healing: *Codependent No More* by Melody Beatty.

The book helped me understand my behavior in relationships, but it was how the book made me feel that had the most impact. I felt seen and heard. And for the first time in a long time, I felt hope.

This newfound empowerment was addictive. I started researching and reading a book a week, exploring various topics like philosophy, psychology, spirituality, law of attraction, and stoicism. I got certifications in different cognitive behavioral techniques and emotional intelligence. And I evolved from being someone who would hide self-help book covers out of embarrassment to someone who would read a bold-titled therapy workbook in public without shame. Unfortunately, like therapy, the techniques in those workbooks were good, but I noticed a lot of gaps and could see that I needed something more to work past the trauma and come back to myself.

So I started making connections, creating hypotheses and testing out new techniques. I saw my mind as a laboratory and I was the test subject. Like the month I prioritized focusing primarily on what I could, could somewhat, and could not control.[3] Or the time I hypothesized that since soldiers who return to their platoons quickly after experiencing a traumatic event are less likely to suffer severe PTSD,[4] maybe if I visualized people helping me in my flashbacks and maladaptive daydreams, the flashbacks and daydreams would go away. They did. Almost instantly.

The night terrors took a little longer to break. But with a combination of Carl Jung's dream theory (which suggests dreams help us tap into our unconscious mind),[5] and the philosophy of trauma specialist Dr. Judith Herman (emphasizing the importance of empowerment in trauma recovery),[6] along with some trial and error, they went away for good in August 2020.

Reflecting on my thoughts and finding new ways to improve my mental health became one of my favorite things to do. Instead of ignoring strange or upsetting thoughts, I'd embrace them and try to understand their meaning. I had fun being creative, inventing new techniques, and experimenting to see what worked. My therapist told me I was speeding through the therapeutic process. It felt good to hear, but the most important thing was that I was coming back to myself.

Life got better in every way, and I wanted to share what I had learned. At work, I led a seminar on emotional intelligence that caught the attention of the human resource department; they asked me to teach it company-wide. In my personal life, friends sought my advice, and I'd guide them toward different perspectives. Witnessing them make connections, think healthier, and rediscover themselves was more rewarding than any financial raise or accolade I had ever received. Motivated to reach a wider audience, I began writing.

Writers in the writing groups loved hearing me break down complex topics in a simple form. One psychologist in the group said he wished all of his colleagues could write about cognitive topics in such a straightforward and approachable way—a skill I contribute to over a decade of explaining complex legal topics to stressed-out sales people who had millions of other things going on and a boss asking about their quota.

Even though there is still so much more for me to learn about psychology and philosophy, in May 2021, I found out that I had learned and experimented enough to go into remission for c-PTSD, depression, and anxiety. Remission means that the symptoms no longer have a significant impact on your life, so you would no longer receive a diagnosis for those conditions. Soon after, I did something I thought I would never do. I let go of the rage that led me on this journey and I forgave the people who mistreated me.

Throughout everything, one thing stayed constant. I kept thinking about the life-changing power of prioritizing healthy and productive thoughts. I strongly believe that by examining our thoughts, we can address common problems people face, such as stress, anxiety, and even physical goals like losing weight. I would go so far as to say that if people paid more attention to creating healthy thoughts, we would solve the mental health crisis and change the world.

With this epiphany, I couldn't shake the feeling that I needed to do something. I really wanted to make something fun and accessible to help people learn this incredible knowledge that saved my life, helped me reconnect with myself, and defy current medical standards. So I left an established career that I spent most of my life building and I started writing books to empower others through thoughts. But to me, this is more than just a book; it's a celebration of how far I've come, all while helping you find yourself again.

BOOK SETUP

The book is split into two sections. Part One teaches you how to recognize unproductive thinking in your mindset and offers a straightforward, yet powerful technique to support your efforts.

In Part Two, you will discover The 7 Rules of Productive Thinking, including additional methods to help calm and reframe your thoughts. Since these techniques are more impactful with practice, I've also included a "template" section at the end of the book. There you will find structured exercises you can use as a supportive thought journal.

IT TAKES TWO

By following these general tips, you'll not only gain valuable insights but also create a journey of personal growth:

- Keeping an open mind helps you build confidence while navigating new topics. Read this book in the voice of a friend who cares about you and wants to see you succeed. This will help you embrace new ideas and ways of thinking.
- Applying what you learn is powerful. The book includes examples and writing activities to enhance your understanding. You don't *have* to

do each writing exercise, but at least thoughtfully consider them.

- Repetition is key for understanding and learning new ideas. Reinforce your learning by practicing exercises and taking notes using the blank pages and spaces throughout the book.

- Growing starts by recognizing what we need to work on. Be honest with yourself when you're thinking about your strengths and weaknesses; this honesty is a powerful tool for personal growth.

- What you learn will help you to better communicate with a therapist. While you can reduce unproductive thoughts without therapy, there is no shame in seeking extra support.

VALUE SETTING

Since thoughts are most productive when aligned with your values,[1] as you work to create more productive thoughts, it's beneficial to use your values, the principles that motivate and drive your decisions, as a guiding force.

Below are twenty personal values. Circle three that resonate with you the most right now. If picking just three seems challenging, keep in mind that one value can lead to another. For example, love may bring friendship and exciting experiences, while success could bring achievements and respect.

Integrity | Adventure | Respect | Justice
Courage | Authenticity | Friendship | Kindness
Spirituality | Compassion | Achievement | Leadership
Loyalty | Independence | Responsibility | Creativity
Love | Honesty | Success | Security

Now, write each selected value and a brief explanation of why it is significant in your life. How does it influence your decisions? What does it represent to you?

Value: _____ is important to me because:

_____

_____

_____

_____

Value: _____ is important to me because:

_____

_____

_____

_____

Value: _____ is important to me because:

_____

_____

_____

_____

Sometimes our thoughts are unproductive because we lose sight of what truly matters to us. We get stuck focusing on trivial things, that deep down, we know we don't really care about. Reconnecting with, and embracing your values, helps you stay focused on what's really important. It will create a level of depth and fulfillment that will reduce stress and help you feel more confident and connected.

While this technique reminded you of your values, it's now up to you to stay tuned in. While seemingly simple, even the most value-driven people can get sidetracked. The key is to continually keep your values front and center by asking questions like, "How does this align with my values?" before making decisions.

THE ROOT CAUSES

PART ONE

Marcus was really looking forward to dinner at his favorite restaurant. When the friendly server told him, "Enjoy your meal," he replied, "You too!" without hesitation.

As soon as the words left his mouth, he felt instant regret and a wave of embarrassment. A simple slip of the tongue quickly snowballed into a whirlwind of thinking. Marcus's thoughts spiraled and his inner critic went into overdrive. *Why did I say that? It was so awkward. The server must think I'm an idiot. I should have just said 'thank you.' What if the server tells the kitchen staff and they are all laughing at me?*

Throughout dinner, Marcus couldn't shake his self-consciousness. He kept replaying the moment in his head, cringing each time he revisited it. He even considered leaving a bigger tip in hopes it would make the server like him.

Later that night, Marcus found himself googling "how to recover from a 'you too' moment." His mind raced as he spent the night reading through countless forum threads with similar stories.

In the days that followed, Marcus kept replaying the incident in his mind. He told himself that people are either good at socializing or they are not, and that he will never be. He wondered if he should avoid going back to that restaurant to save himself from feeling embarrassed. He soon began practicing what he would say if he saw the server again.

———

Poor Marcus. We will use his story to identify the root causes of unproductive thinking and suggest better ways to think. But first, let's talk about thoughts and how we get them in the first place.

THOUGHT BASICS

Understanding how your mind works is key to productive thinking. Instead of feeling confused and stressed, knowing how your thoughts operate allows you to approach uncomfortable and persistent thoughts with curiosity and confidence.

Unfortunately, current information on thoughts can be difficult to grasp; you'll likely need a medical degree or dictionary. Fortunately, when you take away the complex language, thoughts are pretty simple and straightforward. Let's start by focusing on our senses.

Most people have five primary senses: sight, hearing, taste, smell, and touch. These senses help us gather information or "data" from the world around us. Scientists estimate that we absorb 11 million pieces of data every second.[1] Our thoughts are how we become aware of and process this data. Basically, your thoughts are simply how your senses communicate with you. Here are some examples:

- You see a hottie walking past you. You think, *Oh, hello there.*
- The coffee shop you are in turns the music up. You think, *The music sounds louder.*
- You try a new recipe. After tasting the first bite, you think, *This tastes delicious*!
- There's smoke in the air. You notice the smoke and think, *I smell smoke.*
- You try on a new pair of pants. They feel comfortable. You think, *These feel nice.*

Apart from your senses, your thoughts also come from:

- Making connections between ideas, memories, and feelings. Like hearing a song from your childhood and then thinking about your childhood best friend.
- How you feel emotionally. When you're happy, you tend to focus on the good things, but when you're stressed, your thoughts might turn more negative or worried.
- Intentionally directing your thoughts to a particular topic. For instance, focusing on learning about thoughts, as you are doing here.

CONSCIOUS AWARENESS

To handle the vast amount of data gathered from your senses, your brain sorts it using a basic system: information you need to be aware of (conscious) and information you don't need to be aware of (unconscious). Scientists believe that you can consciously process about fifty pieces of data per second, so your unconscious mind takes care of the rest.[2]

What falls into conscious and unconscious awareness varies from person to person, but the main objective is to ensure your safety and focus on what matters to you. Here's the general idea:

UNCONSCIOUS AWARENESS	CONSCIOUS AWARENESS
Something that isn't dangerous and won't harm you (e.g., background noise)	Something that can harm you or is dangerous (e.g., a creeper in an alley)
Something you're not concentrating on (e.g., the person sitting at a table near you at a coffee shop)	Something you're actively thinking about (e.g., a new love interest)
Something you're not actively searching for (e.g., a painting on a wall)	Something you're actively looking for (e.g., your car keys)

You can bring certain things to conscious awareness by actively focusing on them. For example, you might start thinking about the person sitting near you at a coffee shop because it was mentioned above. You might even notice a painting on a building you've walked past many times before but never really seen.

Things can shift from conscious awareness to the unconscious and come back to conscious awareness again. For instance, when you wear comfortable shoes, you'll initially be aware of how comfortable they are. Then other things become more important, and the comfort of your shoes goes to unconscious awareness. But if the shoes start giving you blisters, your attention will return to them.

Conscious awareness is also why you notice the smell of your house when returning from vacation. Every home has a unique scent that, over time, becomes part of your unconscious awareness since you're in your house almost every day. But after being away for some time, you'll likely notice your home's distinct smell because the "nose blind" effect fades.

Another example is locking car doors. With a new car, it takes focus to lock the door. But after doing it a few times, you might find yourself at work wondering if you locked your car before coming in.

Realizing the amount of data that goes into your unconscious mind may feel overwhelming. You might wonder exactly what you aren't aware of and imagine you're missing out on important and potentially life-changing information, or envision your unconscious mind as a mysterious treasure trove you just can't reach. But don't worry. There's a lot of information you don't need to know or pay attention to (why it goes to the unconscious), and when you understand your thoughts and how they

work, you'll have more control over how your mind orga-
nizes the data you collect.

GENERAL BELIEFS

To help sort information into conscious and unconscious
awareness, you develop beliefs. Beliefs are thoughts you
accept as truth and have had often, so they stick with you.
They influence how you think, feel, and act, shaping your
perspectives and responses to various situations. You form
beliefs about various topics like religion, philosophy, poli-
tics, money, or gender roles, and your beliefs can change
based on new experiences or shifts in your perspective.

For example, when you are young and easily influenced
by outside opinions, it is likely you will inherit viewpoints from your parents. These beliefs will significantly
impact your approach to various aspects of life, including
money. Growing up in a household where money was a
source of stress may lead to the belief that money causes
problems and unhappiness. Consequently, you might
face challenges in pursuing financial success or self-sabo-
tage opportunities for financial stability.

But if you get offered a different perspective, say you meet
a wealthy mentor who is happy and fulfilled, their stories
and insights may challenge your negative beliefs about
money. You will start to see money as abundant and
something to be celebrated. This new belief may drive
you to set ambitious goals, take healthy risks, and work
toward achieving financial success.

CORE BELIEFS

You also develop a set of deeply held convictions about yourself, others, and the world known as "core beliefs."[3] These beliefs serve as a target for your thoughts, shaping your perspectives and opinions. Unlike general beliefs, which can be flexible, core beliefs are fundamental to who you are and harder to change.

For instance, someone with the general belief that they're not good at relationships might change their view after experiencing a healthy relationship. But someone with the core belief that they are fundamentally unlovable or unworthy of love will likely struggle forming relationships, or won't try to form relationships at all. When in healthy relationships, they will act in self-sabotaging ways, reinforcing their unhealthy core belief.

Since core beliefs are mostly unconscious, many people aren't aware of them or how they hold them back from reaching their goals. They can carry these convictions throughout their entire lives keeping them stuck as the world evolves around them.

Core beliefs can be positive, negative, or neutral. For example, a negative core belief about relationships is that people are essentially untrustworthy and will always let you down. Someone with this outlook will avoid forming close connections and remain guarded, expecting the worst from others.

On the other hand, someone who holds an optimistic core belief that people are inherently good may approach new acquaintances with warmth and trust in their kindness. This attitude can nurture strong bonds as they are more willing to extend trust and compassion. However, their trusting nature could make them open to manipulation by untrustworthy people.

Lastly, someone with a neutral core belief that people have both positive and negative aspects takes a more neutral approach. They would evaluate each person based on their actions rather than making assumptions or jumping to conclusions.

THOUGHT HABITS

In addition to beliefs, you develop mental patterns called "thought habits" to process information quickly. These unconscious habits affect how you interpret situations, make decisions, and respond to challenges. Similar to physical habits, not all thought habits are healthy; some contribute to mental well-being, while others are harmful.

For example, thought patterns such as optimism and gratitude contribute to mental well-being, while habits like self-doubt and cognitive distortions (which we will explore further in the following chapters) lead to stress.

Due to how conscious and unconscious awareness works, familiar thought patterns, whether good or bad, feel safe and become embedded in your unconscious mind. This is why many people remain unaware of their harmful thought habits. You might have heard the saying that just because something is familiar does not mean it is healthy, and that applies here.

Some thought habits are productive until they're not. For instance, comparative thinking can be beneficial when used to compare different concepts for learning, but becomes detrimental when comparing our lives to others on social media.

PRODUCTIVE THINKING

"Overthinking" indicates that your thoughts are unproductive. Since your thoughts have likely been unproductive for the majority of your life, it's crucial that you get a deep understanding of what productive thinking is. Here we'll use comparative thinking to analyze the differences between productive and unproductive thoughts.

UNPRODUCTIVE THINKING	PRODUCTIVE THINKING
Dwelling on the past	Solutions focused
Criticizing, being hard on, or doubting yourself	Embracing self-compassion and self-acceptance
Taking the blame for things beyond your control	Focusing on what you can control
Worrying about what might happen in the future	Staying in the present moment
Placing blame on external factors or other people	Taking accountability for your words and actions

(continued)

UNPRODUCTIVE THINKING	PRODUCTIVE THINKING
Being stubborn in your thoughts and not considering other viewpoints	Being open to different perspectives and new ways of thinking
Believing that you can't change your situation	Believing in your ability to make meaningful changes
Focusing on what you don't want	Focusing on what you want

Now, let's compare someone with productive thoughts and someone with unproductive thoughts after a breakup and how it impacts their lives.

Toni feels disappointed and defeated after yet another failed relationship. Stuck in constant thought, they wonder if things would've been different if they'd acted differently. Believing they are doomed to be single forever, they dwell on past breakups, finding solace in stories of others who feel the same. They spend most of their time stalking their ex's social media pages and drinking to cope with their disappointment. Even though they reactivated their dating profile, they put in little effort, sending generic messages that rarely get responses.

Dante ended things with his partner after being cheated on. He's heartbroken and spends time with a trusted friend to talk about his feelings. Despite the temptation to believe everyone cheats and he'll be alone forever, he acknowledges the extreme thoughts and the emotional pain he is experiencing. He focuses on both the good and bad of the relationship and believes he can find a loyal partner. Taking time for himself, he gains clarity on what he wants in a relationship and tries online dating again with a more thoughtful approach.

Rather than dwelling on what he doesn't want, which will heighten feelings of loneliness and misery, Dante shows self-compassion and prioritizes his well-being. This mindset shift will make him more enjoyable to be around and increase his chances of attracting a healthy relationship. Think about it, who would *you* be more drawn toward—someone who is miserable or someone who is looking forward to a new relationship?

THOUGHTS LEAD TO ACTIONS AND RESULTS

Toni and Dante experienced different outcomes due to their contrasting thoughts about similar situations. This pattern is also evident in the examples of differing views on money and relationships. It's not a coincidence. Your thoughts influence how you feel, which then impacts your actions and overall results.

Even though your "overthinking" may seem like an annoyance, it is actually helping you. The mental noise led to uncomfortable feelings, pushing you to learn about your thoughts and make them productive. Creating productive thoughts will help you align with your values and goals. This alignment leads to increased happiness and an openness to new opportunities. The process is commonly referred to as the "law of attraction" or "manifestation."

Now, let's get back to Marcus and examine how his fixed mindset, cognitive distortions, and low self-confidence contributed to his repetitive thoughts.

FIXED MINDSET

Everyone has their own unique mindset. It's a mix of their beliefs, thought habits, viewpoints, and perspectives. Marcus's strong reaction is partly due to his "fixed mindset." People with a fixed mindset believe that their abilities and intelligence are predetermined, permanent, and can't be changed. As a result, they tend to stick to what they're good at, fear failure, avoid challenges, and resist trying anything new. This limits their opportunities and leads to unproductive thoughts.

While we all shy away from challenges now and then, someone with a fixed mindset frequently or completely avoids them. They stick to what they know and say things like, "This is just the way I am." They also:

- abandon goals and avoid tasks they aren't immediately good at
- pursue perfection and get upset if things don't go as planned

- set unrealistic expectations and pay excessive attention to minor details
- blow setbacks out of proportion assuming there will be severe consequences
- engage in self-criticism and have a negative internal dialogue
- constantly seek external validation to affirm their self-worth
- dislike activities that require effort, expecting immediate success
- struggle to accept advice or feedback because they see it as a personal attack
- believe success should come easily and give up if it doesn't

Even when presented with new information and differing viewpoints, those with a fixed mindset are unlikely to change their beliefs. For instance, if someone with a fixed mindset thinks that money causes stress, they will view wealthy people as "lucky" rather than acknowledging the possibility that financial success can be the result of hard work.

People with a fixed mindset worry *a lot* about making mistakes. They believe that any misstep means they're not good enough. Since they don't believe they can change, they get stuck. This constant worry keeps them from moving forward, reinforces their fixed way of thinking, and leads to cycles of self-doubt and anxiety. The pursuit of perfection, being hard on themselves, and seeking external validation are coping mechanisms to feel worthy and in control.

With his fixed mindset, Marcus is convinced he can't improve his social skills, fueling perfectionistic tendencies and fear of any social mistakes. When Marcus makes a minor mistake, he is hard on himself and assumes everyone is making fun of him. He sees a social slip as a sign of failure and a reflection of his self-worth, leading to feelings of embarrassment and negative thoughts.

Throughout it all, Marcus is not enjoying the meal he had been looking forward to, and the negativity comes home with him as he looks for validation by reading similar stories online later that night.

GROWTH MINDSET

Contrary to a fixed mindset, a "growth mindset" promotes personal development and productive thinking.[1] Believing you can improve enables you to focus on opportunities and the good in a situation; you'll take action instead of getting stuck in endless worry and fear of failure.

People with a growth mindset understand that abilities can be developed through dedication and hard work. They embrace challenges, see setbacks as opportunities, and are less reliant on external validation. A growth mindset leads to greater resilience, personal growth, and an optimistic outlook. Those with a growth mindset:

- view challenges as opportunities for growth
- recognize that mistakes are part of the learning process
- value progress over perfection
- consider setbacks as temporary obstacles that can be overcome
- practice self-compassion through positive self-talk
- prioritize their opinion of themselves over what others think
- invest effort and practice to improve
- welcome feedback as a valuable tool for improvement
- remain determined to overcome obstacles on their path to success

People with a growth mindset are receptive to new information. They do not get defensive or feel threatened if someone has a different perspective or viewpoint. Since they view mistakes as part of the learning process, they are also less likely to define themselves by their mishaps and use slip-ups as opportunities for growth.

Marcus's response would have been significantly different if he had a growth mindset. A growth mindset would encourage him to see his comment as a learning opportunity. He would ditch the idea that being good at socializing is a fixed trait and trust that, with practice, he can improve his social skills. Focused on progress, Marcus would stop being hard on himself, work to build his confidence from the inside, and look forward to a chance to go to his favorite restaurant again.

Here are some examples of a fixed vs. growth mindset.

Fixed Mindset: Olivia excessively plans her workouts. She wants every detail to be perfect, and the pressure she puts on herself is exhausting. She ends up avoiding the gym and feels constant guilt for ditching her fitness goals.

Growth Mindset: Olivia understands that consistency in exercising is more important than having a "perfect" routine. She gradually amps up her workouts and prioritizes progress.

Fixed Mindset: Luis is beating himself up for tripping over his words at a networking event. Even after it's over, he keeps replaying the awkward exchange in his mind, convincing himself he sucks at socializing and will never be good at networking.

Growth Mindset: Recognizing that it's okay to make social mistakes, Luis laughs at his stumble and slows himself down while speaking to his new acquaintance. After the party, he feels good about correcting himself and is looking forward to next week's event.

Fixed Mindset: Jada relies on external validation in the form of likes and comments on her social media posts. She obsesses over every detail of her posts, constantly checking how many people viewed them, and is hard on herself if she doesn't get a certain number of likes.

Growth Mindset: Jada posts on social media because she genuinely enjoys sharing her thoughts and experiences. She prioritizes her personal expression over seeking approval, and appreciates when people enjoy her content.

Fixed Mindset: David contemplates a career change, but he's worried he will make the wrong choice. He thinks so much about it that he can't decide because he's afraid that one mistake will ruin his future.

Growth Mindset: David accepts that taking on a new job comes with risks, and he might make mistakes. He researches his options, asks for advice, and makes the best decision he can with the information he has. He's confident he can overcome any potential mistakes.

Fixed Mindset: Mina is eager to learn a new language. Since she was a straight A student in school, she assumes it will come naturally to her. When it's more difficult than she expected, she gets frustrated and quits.

Growth Mindset: Mina appreciates that learning a new skill, like a new language, requires hard work and dedication. She commits to a regular study schedule, even when it's challenging, and she views mistakes as opportunities for improvement.

Fixed Mindset: Suresh made a mistake at work and he can't seem to get it off his mind. He's concerned his boss will think he's not good at his job. Overwhelmed, he starts having trouble concentrating on his other responsibilities.
Growth Mindset: Suresh realizes he messed up, but sees it as a chance to learn and grow professionally. He decides to speak to his boss about his mistake, and asks for feedback so he can improve.

Fixed Mindset: Emily is struggling to accept feedback on her project. Even though the feedback was constructive, she took it personally and can't stop thinking about it.
Growth Mindset: Emily is open to receiving feedback on her project and sees it as a helpful way to improve. Instead of feeling attacked, she acknowledges it stung a little, but sees it as a chance to develop her skills.

FROM FIXED TO GROWTH

It is possible to have a growth mindset in one area of your life and a fixed mindset in others. For instance, Marcus may have a fixed mindset with his social skills but a growth mindset when it comes to his career progression.

To shift from a fixed mindset to a growth mindset, it is important to recognize patterns and identify if your fixed mindset is general or only in certain areas. Use the following prompts to identify when a fixed mindset was leading to unproductive thoughts.

Reading the examples above, did a time when you were thinking unproductively because of a fixed mindset come to mind? Describe it below.

_____

_____

_____

_____

_____

How would the situation have been different if you had a growth mindset? What would you be thinking? How would you act? How would that influence the end result?

_____

_____

_____

_____

_____

UNHELPFUL THINKING HABITS

Unhealthy thought patterns known as "cognitive distortions," also played a role in Marcus's response and his intrusive thoughts after saying, "You too!" Despite the intimidating name, "cognitive" is just a fancy word for "thoughts."[1] So cognitive distortions, or "thought distortions," are simply thoughts that skew your perception, making minor problems seem major, triggering self-doubt, worry, sadness, and repetitive thought loops.

Discovered by psychiatrist Aaron T. Beck, the founder of cognitive behavioral therapy (CBT), these patterns were observed in patients with depression and anxiety. Dr. Beck categorized the unhealthy patterns and helped his patients identify them in their thought processes.

The list of cognitive distortions continues to expand, some resources mention ten,[2] while others cite fifteen, and yet another may list twenty. Here, we explore five common cognitive distortions that lead to unproductive thoughts:

1. *Catastrophizing.* Making things seem much worse than they are, or imagining the worst case scenario, like believing one bad test grade will ruin your entire future.

2. *All-or-Nothing Thinking (aka "Black-and-White Thinking").* Viewing things as either good or bad, with no middle ground. For instance, thinking that if you can't run a full marathon, exercising is pointless.

3. *Mind Reading.* Assuming you know what others are thinking without any strong evidence. Like thinking someone doesn't like you because they made a weird face.

4. *Emotional Reasoning.* Believing your feelings are facts and making decisions based on how you feel rather than what you know. For example, thinking you're not ready to give a presentation because you feel anxious.

5. *Should Thinking.* Setting rigid rules for yourself and others using the word "should." For instance, feeling guilty for taking a day off when you're sick because of the belief that you should be working.

While everyone experiences unhealthy thoughts to some extent, those who frequently think with cognitive distortions often have unhealthy thoughts. They perceive their distorted thoughts as truth, accepting negativity as their normal. This hostile worldview creates uncertainty, a sense of being stuck, and an inner turmoil that leaves those with these unhealthy patterns seeing the world as a scary and hopeless place.

BALANCED THOUGHTS

To prevent cognitive distortions from influencing your perception, it's crucial to create balanced thoughts.[3] This involves maintaining a rational and objective perspective while considering various viewpoints and not going to extremes. Balanced thinking promotes clarity, wise decision-making, and healthier relationships, enabling you to maintain a positive outlook and manage life's challenges without losing your cool.

People with balanced thinking are compassionate and kind to themselves. They accept that their thoughts may become distorted at times. When faced with difficulties, they stay practical, and:

- view situations realistically, instead of blowing them out of proportion
- acknowledge that things aren't black and white and there are shades of gray
- recognize that making assumptions is unproductive
- make decisions on facts rather than solely relying on their feelings
- embrace flexibility and avoid rigid rules

Now, let's see how Marcus was influenced by cognitive

distortions and how a balanced approach would have changed his experience:

- Marcus is **catastrophizing** by thinking that his minor mishap was a significant issue and that the server and kitchen staff are making fun of him. Balanced thinking would prompt Marcus to realize his comment was an innocent mistake. Instead of making it seem worse than it was, he would remind himself that mistakes happen.

- Seeing social interactions as either perfect or a disaster, and thinking he's either really good or really bad at socializing, is **all-or-nothing thinking.** If Marcus balanced his thoughts, he would see that there's a middle ground and that saying "You too!" doesn't mean he's terrible at socializing.

- When Marcus assumes he knows what the server and kitchen staff are thinking about him, even though he doesn't have any proof, he is **mind reading.** With a balanced approach, Marcus wouldn't assume he knows what the server is thinking and would remind himself that people who work in service deal with all kinds of customers every day.

- Marcus thinks the situation is worse than it is because he feels embarrassed. He is confusing feelings for facts, which is a sign of **emotional reasoning.** If he balanced his thoughts, Marcus would separate feelings from reality. Instead of thinking his embarrassment means he made a mistake, he'd know it's normal to feel silly after a little social slip.

- When Marcus criticizes himself, thinking he should have just said "thank you," he is creating rigid rules and **should thinking**. With balanced thoughts, he'd let go of the "shoulds" and understand that he's human and makes mistakes, just like everyone else.

Here are some additional examples of cognitive distortions in action:

Catastrophizing: After making a small typo in a work email, Anthony starts imagining the worst possible outcome. He's worried that his boss might get angry and even consider letting him go. **Balanced Thinking:** Anthony understands that it's okay to make small mistakes and doesn't believe his boss will make a big deal out of it. Instead of dwelling on the worst-case scenario, he simply corrects the error and moves on, trusting that he's good at his job.

All-or-Nothing Thinking: Sarah has big career aspirations, but when she encounters even a small obstacle, she believes her entire future is in jeopardy. This leads her to dwell on her decisions and worry that she'll never succeed. **Balanced Thinking:** Sarah accepts that setbacks are a natural part of working toward your goals. She doesn't let minor issues derail her entire future, but instead uses them as learning opportunities to adjust her plans and keep pushing ahead.

Mind Reading: Alvaro thinks his friends secretly don't like him because they didn't include him in plans. He constantly imagines what they are thinking and assumes they excluded him on purpose.

Balanced Thinking: Alvaro doesn't spend time making up scenarios or assuming why he wasn't included. He reaches out to his best friend, asks about their plans, and says he'd like to join next time.

Emotional Reasoning: Before a social event, Mike is nervous he will say something dumb. He confuses his feelings as facts and believes that his nervousness means he will definitely say something offensive.

Balanced Thinking: Mike isn't overly concerned about saying the wrong thing. He knows that everyone makes mistakes in conversations, and most people are understanding. Rather than trying to predict what other people will think, he focuses on meeting new people.

Should Thinking: Yan feels like she should please everyone and make them happy. So, when she can't go to her friend's party because of work, she feels bad for not living up to her own "should" standards.

Balanced Thinking: Yan knows that her work is important and what she needs to focus on. She talks to her friend, says she's sorry she can't make it, and suggests another time to hang out. She doesn't put pressure on herself to please everyone all the time.

CREATING BALANCE

Cognitive distortions often go unnoticed because they are unconscious habits. Bringing these distortions to conscious awareness involves identifying instances when you previously had distortions in your thinking, and challenging the distorted thoughts with new perspectives and evidence.

During the process it's beneficial to identify the specific cognitive distortions at play, so you can determine what distortions are most common in your mindset. From there, repetition is key. These distortions have likely been influencing your thoughts since early childhood. Correcting them requires consistent repetition and time.

As you were reading the examples, did you recall a time when you were thinking with distorted thoughts? Describe the situation in detail. What were your thoughts at that time? What types of cognitive distortions were present?

_____

_____

_____

_____

_____

Do you have any evidence to support your thoughts? What evidence can you find that proves they aren't true?

_____

_____

_____

_____

_____

TIP: To help determine fact from assumption it can be helpful to imagine you are giving advice to a friend in the same situation.

How would the situation look with balanced thoughts? How would balanced thoughts influence your emotional reaction and response?

_____

_____

_____

_____

_____

LOW SELF-CONFIDENCE

Marcus's response also reveals a lack of confidence in social situations. While occasional self-doubt is common, those with low confidence have persistent doubts about themselves and their abilities. They often think other people are superior and know things they don't.

Low confidence can stem from various sources, such as a lack of experience or past disappointments. For example, someone who made a poor investment choice may hesitate when making further financial decisions.

Criticism from others can also lead to low confidence and cause someone to develop a negative self-image. For instance, if someone is passionate and excited about pursuing a career or artistic endeavor, and others make fun of them or call their ideas dumb, they may internalize the negative opinions and abandon their goals.

Low self-confidence can create a cycle of self-doubt and

unproductive thoughts, leading those with low confidence to:

- question their choices and abilities, doubting if they can achieve goals
- avoid trying new things and fear making mistakes
- criticize themselves and question if they deserve happiness
- seek external validation to feel good about themselves
- feel deeply hurt by criticism, interpreting it as a reflection of their worth
- struggle to accept compliments because they don't believe them
- compare themselves to others and feel like they're inferior
- avoid talking about their achievements
- isolate out of fear of judgment or feeling unworthy

While confidence itself isn't exactly thinking, your level of confidence is influenced by your thought patterns. Reframing your thoughts in a more confident manner will help you build a more productive and confident mindset. This positive outlook removes the urge to keep fixating on your mistakes and flaws.

While confident people doubt themselves sometimes, they typically have faith in their abilities, which helps them handle tough situations. Confident people focus on finding solutions and learning from their mistakes; they don't get stuck in "what ifs." This looks like:

- having faith in your choices and ability to overcome challenges
- trying new things and trusting you can handle whatever comes your way
- practicing self-compassion and prioritizing self-love
- focusing on internal validation
- appreciating criticism and using it to improve
- accepting compliments in stride
- embracing individuality and remembering that everyone has their own unique strengths
- celebrating achievements and support from others
- feeling comfortable in social situations without fear of judgment

It's important to acknowledge that confidence levels may vary in different parts of life. And while you may be confident in certain areas, you might not be confident in a decision you made in that area. For example, you may feel confident when it comes to dating and personal relationships, but doubt a hasty judgment you made, or feel uncertain when dealing with interview situations or speaking to the CEO.

People can also experience lapses in confidence in specific situations, which is possibly what happened during Marcus's mishap. Let's consider how things would have turned out if he had acted more confidently.

If Marcus had higher confidence in social situations, he might feel a bit awkward for saying "you too" but he wouldn't question his social skills. He would quickly realize that making silly mistakes, like saying something clumsy, can happen to anyone. Instead of being hard on himself, Marcus wouldn't be overly critical. He would focus on enjoying his meal rather than worrying about what the server thought of him. Marcus might even find humor in the situation and instead of considering avoiding his favorite restaurant, he would think of the situation as an opportunity to connect with the server in the future.

Here are some examples of confidence in action:

Low Confidence: Sasha is feeling uneasy about her social interactions. She often dwells on the things she said, concerned about how others perceive her. She's also curious if she may have unintentionally upset someone or misinterpreted certain remarks.

Confidence: Sasha is genuine and straightforward when communicating with others, without analyzing every word she says. She trusts that her friends appreciate her for being herself and doesn't stress about potentially offending anyone.

Low Confidence: James is nervous people won't accept or include him. When he's invited to social

events, he often wonders if the invitation is out of pity or obligation rather than genuine interest.
Confidence: James knows that he's an important part of his friend group, and he doesn't dwell on why he's included in gatherings. Instead, he just considers if he wants to go or not.

Low Confidence: Cody isn't too sure about his looks and spends a good amount of time thinking about what to wear while checking himself out in the mirror.
Confidence: Cody focuses on his opinion of himself and the things he can do to feel good about how he looks. He doesn't spend too much time in front of the mirror and he picks his clothes based on what he likes and feels comfortable in.

Low Confidence: Nushi struggles with decision-making, particularly when it involves taking care of herself. She constantly second-guesses her food choices, fitness routine, and overall lifestyle, leading to feelings of anxiety and frustration.
Confidence: Nushi trusts she'll make smart decisions when it comes to food, staying active, and taking care of her health. She's committed to making better choices and doesn't stress because she knows she's doing her best.

Low Confidence: Vera often feels uncertain about her job and where she wants to take her career. She's always weighing different career options and worries that she might not be qualified for a promotion.

Confidence: Vera is not sure how her career will turn out, but she focuses on what she enjoys and makes decisions while believing in herself and that she deserves to advance in her job.

MAKING CONFIDENCE

When it comes to building confidence, the phrase "Fake it till you make it" is often misunderstood. Contrary to popular belief, it doesn't mean pretending to be confident until you achieve a specific goal. It means adopting confident behaviors and attitudes until you genuinely feel confident in yourself and your abilities.

The fun part is, when you build confidence in one area, you can leverage it to feel more confident in others. You would think, *I achieved a really difficult goal; I can do these new goals too!*

In Marcus's situation, "Fake it till you make it" would involve Marcus acting like he was confident in social situations, even if he feels uncertain. He would continue to go to the restaurant, and engage in social interactions to feel more assured while socializing.

To build confidence, think of previous situations where you didn't have trust in your abilities, and consider how you could have acted more confidently. Reflecting on previous experiences gives you the space to recognize how you can confidently manage similar situations in the future. Remember, even the most confident person experiences moments of self-doubt.

Use the following prompts to identify areas where you can nurture self-confidence.

When you read the examples above, did you recall a time you weren't feeling very sure of yourself? Describe the situation. What were you thinking at that time?

_____

_____

_____

_____

_____

How would the situation be different if you showed confidence? What would you be thinking then?

_____

_____

_____

_____

_____

TIP: It can be helpful to imagine you are giving advice to a friend in a similar situation.

THE CHANGE PROCESS

To develop productive thoughts, you need to focus on a process called "cognitive restructuring." Although it may sound complicated, remember that "cognitive" is just a fancy word for thoughts. So, in simple terms, cognitive restructuring means you are changing the way you think.

Consider it a thought upgrade. You're unlearning unproductive thought patterns and adopting new, more effective ways of thinking. You've already started this process in the previous chapters, but now we'll go into more details. Here is a full look at the cognitive restructuring process:

- *Step 1: Awareness.* The initial step involves recognizing the unhelpful thoughts that are holding you back. Developing awareness requires reflection on past instances of "overthinking" and the unproductive thoughts in those situations.

- *Step 2: Identify the Thoughts.* Once you are aware of the unhelpful thoughts, or root causes, you pinpoint the specific thought habits or patterns that led to the repetitive and unproductive thoughts.
- *Step 3: Challenge and Replace.* From there you challenge the thoughts by asking questions like:
  - "Is this thought based on truth or just an assumption?"
  - "What evidence do I have for or against this thought?" and
  - "Is there a more balanced way to see this situation? What might that be?"

For example, Amina realizes that she thinks with cognitive distortions, like all-or-nothing thinking. One day, she noticed she forgot to attach a file to an email and caught herself thinking, "I always mess things up." Aware that this mindset wasn't healthy, she changed her thinking to, "I make mistakes sometimes; this is a small one and I caught it quickly." She sent the attachment in a follow-up email and started looking forward to the weekend. Every now and then, the mistake would cross her mind, but she would remind herself that she caught it quickly and there was nothing left to think about.

Awareness is the first step. Even if Amina didn't immediately catch her all-or-nothing thinking, becoming aware of the unhealthy thought afterwards still sets her on the right path. Reflecting on the unproductive thought allows her to consider how she might have responded differently had she noticed it in the moment. The more you practice reflection, the more you build self-awareness, and the quicker you will notice unproductive thoughts in real time.

Even people who have developed and consistently use these techniques (like me) still occasionally have unproductive thoughts slip through. It can happen when you're tired or stressed, sometimes it just happens randomly. The key is not allowing perfection to get in the way of progress; when you do catch an unproductive thought—whether days or years later—it's important to celebrate your growth.

While this process may seem straightforward, it can be difficult in practice because you've likely had your thought habits for a long time. It takes courage to recognize and constantly challenge your thoughts. Some might find it hard to admit they have unhealthy thought patterns in the first place, believing it will make them seem flawed. They may first have to work through denial and perfectionism before addressing their thoughts directly.

THE ICE METHOD

Improving the way you think isn't just about stopping unproductive thoughts; it's a valuable skill that will have a positive impact on your mental and emotional well-being. The ICE Method offers an easy approach to cognitive restructuring by helping you identify, challenge, and evaluate "hot" thoughts.

Hot thoughts are the unproductive thoughts we've been talking about. They are strong, negative thoughts that, while irrational, can trick you into seeing yourself and the world in a negative light.[1] Hot thoughts can make you feel bad, upset, or act in ways that are counter to your goals. Ever felt like you couldn't control your emotions or been too hard on yourself? That's likely because of a hot thought.

Hot thoughts stem from unhelpful thinking habits or an unhealthy mindset. While we can't stop these thoughts from occurring, changing how we perceive them weakens their power over us. The more we cool these hot thoughts down, the less frequently they'll trouble our minds.

The ICE Method involves three simple steps:

1. Identifying the hot thoughts
2. Challenging and changing the hot thoughts to make them healthier
3. Evaluating how reframing the hot thoughts will improve your life

The great news is, you're already using the ICE Method! We applied this approach in the introduction when we *identified* how unproductive it is to judge thoughts on an over/under scale, *challenged* that "hot" thought by focusing on making thoughts productive, and *evaluated* how productive thoughts will lead to a more fulfilling life. You've also been working on the first two steps—identifying and challenging hot thoughts—in the last few chapters.

To keep the momentum going, let's focus on evaluation. The cognitive restructuring process can be challenging at times. Even with dedication and giving your all, staying motivated can be a struggle. Evaluation helps you stay on track.

When we evaluate, we look at three things:

1. *Actions you can take to improve the situation.* Sometimes we get stuck in unproductive thoughts because we need to take action to improve the situation we are stuck thinking about.

2. *How reducing hot thoughts helps you reach your goals and how good that will feel.* Imagining positive feelings and the benefits of correcting hot thoughts will boost your motivation, even if you don't see immediate results.

3. *The things that are stopping you from changing.* Sometimes, we hold onto unhelpful thoughts because they are serving a purpose. When we evaluate, we figure out how these thoughts "help" us, and then look for healthier alternatives.

Let's work on the evaluation portion now. Since you are already taking action by reading this book and creating more productive thoughts, we will focus on the last two pieces. Think about what you learned in the past three chapters.

How good will it feel to reduce "overthink" and create more productive thoughts?

_____

_____

_____

_____

_____

How will reframing your thoughts help you stay better aligned with your values and goals?

_____

_____

_____

_____

_____

How was your unproductive thinking serving you? How was it hurting you?

_____

_____

_____

_____

_____

ICING UNPRODUCTIVE THOUGHTS

Now let's bring it all together and use the ICE Method to identify and challenge unproductive thinking in general.

Identify

When you took the quiz and read about the signs of unproductive thinking in the Introduction, what resonated with you? In what situations do you tend to think unproductively the most? Can you identify any of the root causes in your mindset?

_____

_____

_____

_____

_____

_____

How is unproductive thinking negatively impacting you and keeping you from your goals?

_____

_____

_____

_____

_____

_____

Challenge

Instead of sticking with your current mindset and
thought patterns, what are alternative and more productive ways to think?

_____

_____

_____

_____

Evaluate

How will creating productive thoughts positively impact
you and help you prioritize your values and goals?

_____

_____

_____

_____

How has unproductive thinking been serving you? Is
thinking about something continually giving you a sense
of empowerment? Are you using your thoughts in an
attempt to avoid your feelings or feel in control? Is over-
analyzing an attempt to be perfect? Are you trying to
avoid difficult conversations?

_____

_____

_____

_____

_____

How will facing your feelings, leaning into imperfection, and improving your thoughts help you get back to yourself and benefit you in the long run?

_____

_____

_____

_____

Understanding how your mind works and the cognitive restructuring process is a significant stride in reducing unproductive thinking. Just learning about this process can make you feel more powerful and in control of your thoughts.

While the ICE Method is here to help you identify and correct unhelpful thoughts, it's up to you to keep practicing it. The more you reframe your thoughts, the less mental noise you'll have. And the more you challenge past thoughts, the easier reframing your thoughts will become. Eventually, you'll find yourself naturally replacing unproductive thoughts with healthier thoughts in real time.

Here are some tips to speed up the process:

- *Be Kind to Yourself.* When you are hard on yourself, you slow down the process. To build self-compassion, ask yourself what you would say to a friend in a similar situation.

- *Be Patient and Persistent.* Changing thought patterns requires practice. Keep reflecting on past situations and eventually you will be able to change thoughts in real time. Even if you work through an unproductive thought pattern, it might come back during stressful times. Be patient with yourself. Remember that setbacks are a sign of progress. Noticing setbacks means you are aware of how you can improve, which means you soon will.

- *Seek Support.* Outside support can offer different perspectives. If you find yourself having trouble or feel stuck, reach out to a trusted friend, mentor, or coach, or consider counseling with a therapist or counselor.

- *Keep a Thought Journal.* Writing your thoughts down will diminish their power and help you track your progress. Templates and blank sheets are available at the end of this book. Alternatively, you can get a dedicated notebook or journal.

- *Use Mindfulness and Other Supportive Techniques.* Certain methods will help you view your thoughts more objectively, making it easier to reframe them. Let's explore these in Part Two.

THE 7 RULES OF PRODUCTIVE THINKING
PART TWO

Here we'll explore common thought techniques and some unique strategies I've developed to support you in creating productive thoughts. You will also learn some fresh perspectives and useful tips for learning and practicing these techniques. Think of it like building a strong structure. Focusing on the root causes first is like laying the foundation. The techniques in this section are the support beams.

Instead of listing the techniques one by one, I've grouped them into sections called "The 7 Rules of Productive Thinking." If one or a few rules resonate with you, or feel like something you need to work on, you can use the title of the section as an affirmation.

Affirmations are short reminders you can say to yourself to feel confident and stay focused. They're easy to repeat, which helps you internalize their message. To get the most out of them, repeat each affirmation ten times every day before bed and when you wake up. This reinforces what you've learned and keeps it fresh in your mind. I've personally used each of these rules as an affirmation at one point or another, occasionally saving them as my phone background for a friendly reminder.

RULE #1: I AM THE OBSERVER

In a study conducted at the University of Virginia, participants were given the choice to either sit quietly with their thoughts or give themselves an electric shock. Most participants opted for the electric shock, emphasizing the discomfort many of us feel when we're alone with our thoughts. Why are we all so uncomfortable?

The study's moderators suggest that, "most people seem to prefer to be doing something rather than nothing, even if that something is negative."[1] And while boredom may be a factor, there appears to be a deeper issue at play. Most people feel uneasy with their thoughts because they have been conditioned to closely identify with them. When faced with a strange or unkind thought, they tend to believe it defines their identity, but that's not reality.

You are not your thoughts; you observe them. Your thoughts are your advocates, meant to keep you safe and help you achieve goals. They are not something you need to escape from. The more comfortable you feel sitting with and observing your thoughts, the easier it will be to create productive thought habits.

YOU ARE NOT YOUR THOUGHTS

Thoughts are your awareness of the information your senses send you. You are aware of the data, not the data itself.

A simple way to show that you are separate from your thoughts is to compare thinking to dreaming.[2] Just like everyone has thoughts, everyone dreams. And just like you are not your dreams, you are not your thoughts, you are the observer of them. So instead of saying "I think, therefore I am," a more accurate phrase would be "I think, therefore I can observe my thoughts;" or "I think, therefore I am conscious of my thoughts."

Uncomfortable thoughts often create unease because they don't align with who you truly are. The discomfort is your gut alerting you to this misalignment with your values or goals.

By not identifying with your thoughts, you won't feel the need to avoid them. Instead, you'll give yourself space to challenge uncomfortable thoughts and ask, "Why doesn't this feel right?" It could be a strange idea from a TV show, stemming from anxiety, or influenced by someone projecting their fears onto you.

INTRUSIVE THOUGHTS

Something that doesn't get much attention (probably because people assume they are their thoughts) is the fact that it's normal to have strange, unsettling, or unconventional thoughts known as "intrusive thoughts." We all get them—even that person you most admire. Even Keanu Reeves and Oprah! There are several types of intrusive thoughts, including:

- random and unsettling ideas that seem to come from nowhere, like imagining harming yourself or others even though you have no intention of doing so
- irrational fears or phobias that don't make sense, like having an intense fear of harmless animals, everyday objects, or common situations, such as riding an elevator
- unusual desires, like having preferences that go against social norms, making you feel uneasy or embarrassed

But it's not the thoughts that matter, it's what you do with them. Rather than pushing away or ignoring intrusive thoughts, acknowledging their strangeness, and approaching them with curiosity will diminish their influence, empowering you in the process.

WATCHING THEM PLAY OUT

A way to deal with anxious and intrusive thoughts is to let them run their course, or watch them "play out." Allowing thoughts to play out keeps you from getting stuck in *what ifs*. For example, I used to have troubling thoughts about friends and family passing away. It made me sad, and I would often end up in tears. It felt dark, but I started to let the thoughts play out. I would think about how I'd feel if the person I was imagining dying actually passed away. What would I do for their funeral? What would I miss about them? How would I manage my grief? I even considered how much time I would need to take off work.

The more I played the thoughts out, the quicker they stopped. With a clearer mind, I realized that I was scared of losing a specific person because I loved them. If I met someone new and started to worry about losing them, I would think, "Wow, I really care about them!" and the anxious thoughts would dissipate. Now, because of this work, I've come to a point where I can love someone without the fear of losing them.

You can try this method with common anxious thoughts, like losing your job or doing something you do not actually plan on doing. If you are nervous you are going to lose your job, ask yourself: How much money do I have saved up? Will I need to move in with a friend or my parents? What kind of work could I find? If you are having anxious thoughts of doing something unfavorable —let's say you're at a concert and you start to worry about what it would be like to jump into the crowd from the balcony—you would ask: How many people would I land on? How far would I fall? Would I get hurt? What is triggering my anxiety and keeping me from focusing on the concert?

WHAT IS THIS REALLY ABOUT?

Sometimes thoughts are there to teach us a lesson or keep us safe, even if they don't make sense. To deal with unusual, intrusive thoughts, approach them with curiosity and look for the lessons they might hold. Embarrassed to share this, but here is an example from my life to show what it's like to manage intrusive thoughts with curiosity.

I was dating someone who would commonly call women "crazy." Eventually he started calling me crazy too. Even though the relationship was short-lived, I could not get the idea of him calling me "crazy" out of my mind. I started having intrusive thoughts and irrational worries of him coming to my house with the police, telling the police I was crazy and the police taking me away.

The thoughts were incredibly uncomfortable and bizarre, but instead of trying to ignore them, I faced them with curiosity. Why does my brain lead me to think I might get admitted to an insane asylum? Being triggered by an insult is about the insult itself, not the person saying it. So, why does the term "crazy" upset me?

It did not come immediately, but one day, I found my answer. I remembered when I was a kid, my grandmother, who grew up in a time when women would be admitted to insane asylums for questionable reasons, like not having the same religion as their husband, would repeatedly tell me to never let someone think I was crazy or I would be admitted. Completely unaware, her fear became mine, and these intrusive thoughts were my mind's way of keeping me safe.

To ease the intensity of the intrusive thoughts, I reminded myself that I live in a different time, the unethical practices my grandmother was afraid of, and the fear she projected onto me, is not rational. With that clarity, I realized the women that guy was talking about weren't "crazy;" they were stressed out from his mixed messages. It helped me realize how much I appreciate and enjoy consistency in relationships. The intrusive thoughts gradually dissipated.

THE TV WATCHER (AKA THE HOMER SIMPSON)

A simple technique that can help you sit with your thoughts resembles being a TV watcher. You "change the channel" on your unwanted or intrusive thoughts. It goes like this:

> **Self-Critical:** Everyone at this party thinks you're weird. *Hmm, that's not nice. I'd rather think something else.*

Less Self-Critical: Some people at this party think you are weird. *All right, that's better, but what else?*
Self-Compassionate: You're weird in an awesome way and will find your people. *Okay, that's much better. I like this.*

THOUGHTS ARE YOUR FRIENDS

Approaching your thoughts with curiosity will help you discover how truly valuable they are. Sometimes it's as simple as telling your critical or negative thoughts you don't have time for them. Like when I was writing this book, I started doubting myself, but I knew I was committed to pushing forward. I told myself, "I don't have time for this right now," and the negative thoughts went away.

As you challenge unhelpful thinking patterns and build productive thoughts, it is important to recognize the difference between the discomfort of learning something new, which diminishes over time, and a thought that doesn't align with who you are. You can figure this out by asking yourself how the discomfort feels.

Does it make you grow and feel challenged (maybe a little curious and excited), or does it create inner conflict and disharmony? It gets easier to tell the difference between the two as you pay closer attention to your thought processes.

RULE #2: I LIVE IN THE PRESENT

We're often encouraged *not* to live in the present moment. We're pressured to think about the past with comments like, "If only you had done things differently," and "Life was so much better in the good old days." And we are taught to worry about the future, with questions like, "What if it doesn't work out?" or "What if something goes wrong?"

This constant pressure makes it hard to appreciate life. It also causes a lot of stress and shows us why "overthinking" is closely linked to depression and anxiety. If you keep dwelling on the past, you'll miss the good that is happening and end up feeling depressed. And if you're hyper-focused on the future, you'll get stuck in worry and feel anxious.

But the past is gone, the future is unknown, and the present moment is all you truly have.[1] So if you want to create productive thoughts, and stop the constant rumination and worry, you need to prioritize living in the now.

THE ART OF ACTION

Constant focus on the past and future trains our minds to dwell and stress. Rumination and worry become an unconscious habit. Mindfulness techniques are often recommended to break this cycle, and in certain situations mindfulness techniques are helpful, but oftentimes the most effective thing you can do is *take action*.

This means replacing habitual thinking with actions that will help you improve. For example, instead of wondering if someone likes you, simply ask them, "Hey, I think you're fun. Want to get a cup of coffee?" If the idea of asking someone to hang out makes you nervous, take action by stepping out of your comfort zone. Express your interests directly or practice asking for what you want in front of a mirror or with a supportive friend.

Exploring various actions to live in the present moment opens the door to productive thinking. Here are some examples:

1. Instead of continually thinking about everyday decisions like what to eat and wear, try finding simple meals and outfits you enjoy. Screenshot recipes and take pictures when you wear your favorite outfits. Save the pictures to an album on your phone so you can easily refer to them when you need to decide what to wear or eat.

2. Instead of worrying about a health concern, focus on incorporating foods that are good for that issue into your diet. When you eat those

foods, think, *I am doing my best to help my body thrive.* Make sure to see a doctor as needed.

3. Instead of feeling overwhelmed by your "to-do" list, look for ways to make tasks easier. Find ways to streamline, use a password manager, and get in the habit of doing tasks that take less than ten minutes as soon as they come to mind.

4. Instead of stressing about how you sound and come across in conversations, consider how you ideally want to act in different situations. Watch videos to improve your speaking style and ask trusted friends for feedback.

5. Instead of getting anxious about how to get promoted, research the next steps in your career. Ask your boss about your career path and make a plan for the next six months with clear steps. Alternatively, update your resume and start applying for new jobs.

6. Instead of focusing on whether someone likes you or if they will call, figure out what you want and need in a relationship. Ask yourself if this person is a good fit and think about what you can do to be an amazing partner and friend.

7. Instead of feeling stuck and like you "overthink everything," use the ICE Method to identify what situations you think about most and work to create more productive thoughts around those situations.

There are a lot of actions you can take to live in the present moment, and the more you practice, the easier it becomes. Don't forget that living in the present moment could be as straightforward as allowing yourself to relax without guilt. Maybe you've been yearning to pursue a lifelong dream or try a new hobby? Remember, you can enjoy hobbies without turning them into a business.

PERMISSION NOT TO THINK

If thinking is a habit, it keeps you stuck. You might struggle to decide what to eat because you are in the habit of thinking instead of simply choosing something. But it's important to give yourself permission to embrace simplicity. It's okay not to think. You have permission to make simple choices, like what to eat or wear, without constantly analyzing them.

You are allowed not to dwell on embarrassing moments. If someone brings up something awkward you said, it's okay to respond with honesty and humor, saying, "Yeah, I say dumb things sometimes."

You have permission not to obsess over what others think of you or replay and analyze past interactions. It's okay to simply enjoy the moment for what it was. You're allowed to enjoy a date and simply think, *That was fun; they were nice.*

You're allowed not to dwell on arguments. Instead of defining yourself by a disagreement, give yourself permission to apologize and move forward, even if others don't accept your apology.

You have permission not to have your entire future mapped out. It's okay not to have a detailed plan for the next five years. Most people with a five year plan don't stick to that plan anyway. Instead, focus on growth and discovery along the way.

You're allowed not to carry the weight of the world on your shoulders. Protect your mental well-being by giving yourself permission not to constantly worry about global events. Instead, focus on making a positive impact in your own community. It can be as simple as giving your neighbors friendly greetings.

MINDFULNESS

Living in the now can also look like allowing yourself to relax without thought. A common mindfulness technique that will help you focus on the present and improve your ability to manage unwanted thoughts is a bit like daydreaming. For this technique, you imagine your thoughts as something you can touch, then watch them float away.

Typically, this visualization is done with leaves falling from trees into a peaceful river. You imagine standing by the riverbank and picture leaves falling from the trees into the water. Now, imagine your thoughts as those falling leaves. Watch them float away with the river until they disappear from sight.

Alternatively, you can apply this technique with other concrete objects, like balloons floating away, sushi moving on a conveyor belt in a restaurant, or clouds drifting in the sky. Personally, I like to envision a thought as a nondescript object in my hand. With a swift motion, I release the thought into the air, then I excitedly look up toward the sky while taking a deep breath.

EMBRACING THE NOW

Embracing the present moment is essential for maintaining mental health and overall well-being. Prioritizing the now will not only help you think productively, it also reduces stress and helps you plan for the future. Instead of dwelling on past mistakes, or anxiously anticipating the unknown future, you will fully embrace the richness of your experiences and relationships.

Living in the present does not mean neglecting responsibilities or dismissing the value of planning. Rather, it involves finding a balance between learning from the past, planning for the future, and appreciating the present moment. This holistic approach empowers you to make better decisions, appreciate the journey, and navigate life's twists and turns with resilience.

So, the next time you find yourself caught up in the past, or overwhelmed by worries about the future, remind yourself of the importance of embracing the now. Life unfolds in this very moment, and by being fully present, you put yourself in a position to seize the opportunities it offers.

RULE #3: I AM MY OWN HERO

Most of us are conditioned to prioritize the needs of others, often believing that if we make other people happy, we'll be happy too. We are encouraged to find "The One," or a person who will complete us and rescue us from our lives. We convince ourselves that if we do the right things or wait just long enough, then that perfect person will come along.

This fixation leads us to neglect our own well-being, leaving us feeling powerless and unfulfilled. We forget about ourselves, and to avoid facing the sadness of our self-abandonment, we stay busy with unproductive thoughts, rumination, and worry. But you do not need to wait for someone to save you. Truth is, you are the only one who gets to save yourself. And while that may sound daunting, it's actually incredibly rewarding.

Becoming the person you need not only creates productive thoughts, it fosters happiness in yourself and those around you. By prioritizing your own needs, you empower yourself to live a fulfilling life, positively impacting others along the way.

THE SELFISHNESS MYTH

We've been sold the lie that focusing on ourselves is selfish and "bad." This misguided belief is a result of all-or-nothing thinking. It shows us that people have forgotten they can focus on themselves while still caring about others. Truth is, prioritizing your needs not only builds self-love, it creates a compassion you will share with others. You'll also be happier and more fun to be around.

If you haven't focused on your needs before, advocating for yourself can seem scary. By focusing on others for so long, you may not even know what your needs are. You might even worry about being labeled as "needy."

But it is essential to recognize that asking for your needs does not make you demanding or high-maintenance. It's a celebration of you prioritizing yourself, and it's an important part of self-care.

Someone might think your needs are too much, but that doesn't mean you're *too* needy. It just shows that you're not a good match for each other, or that they're not willing or able to meet you where you are. It's not personal, it's about compatibility.

While it's possible you may have unrealistic expectations in some areas—likely because of unrealistic storylines portrayed on TV and in the media—you can always adjust your expectations if you are not getting the results you hoped for. In my experience, those who confide in me about their challenges in expressing their needs usually have reasonable requests.

Personally, some people have thought I was "too needy" because I like to make plans in advance. But, by staying true to myself, I've found genuine connections with people who share similar preferences, and I had the regimented schedule I needed to write this book.

HAVING NEEDS ISN'T NEEDY

Instead of prioritizing other people's needs, it's essential to focus on your own. To be your own hero, consider the following steps:

1. Figure out what you truly want and practice asking for it. Do you really want the gigantic mansion with fancy furniture or do you simply want a comfortable place where you can relax with loved ones?
2. Identify what your ideal relationships would look like and focus on nurturing connections that add value to your life. Do you really need someone with a certain look, or would you find stronger connections with people who have similar values?
3. Strive to become someone you're proud of, independent of other people's opinions. When you look at yourself in the mirror, are you proud?

If not, what steps can you take to cultivate self-pride?

4. Take ownership of your actions, acknowledging mistakes, and committing to growth. It can be as simple as admitting, "I am embarrassed by this, but I…" and then working to do better in the future.

5. Ditch the idea of perfection and focus on personal growth without the pressure. Since perfection is unattainable, what can you do to be the best version of yourself?

6. Embrace an abundance mindset. Recognize that there are always new opportunities and people out there. If limitations were removed, what would you want to do with your life? How can you work toward that now?

7. Set clear boundaries and assertively communicate them. In what relationships do you find you lose yourself the most? That is where boundaries are most needed.

THE PRIMARY GOALS

We're all in different stages in our lives, so goals will naturally be different for each of us, but there are some primary goalposts we all need to keep in mind:

- Focus on what you want instead of what you *don't* want—like we are doing here in prioritizing productive thinking instead of just "stopping overthinking."

- Continually remind yourself that progress takes time.
- Practice patience with yourself and take time to celebrate small wins.
- Try to be consistent, but don't get discouraged if you miss a few days. Remember that one or two bad days don't erase months of progress and hard work.
- Learn from mistakes and be willing to modify your goals based on new information and changes in your life.

PERSONAL BOUNDARIES

Boundaries, the guidelines you create to tell other people how to connect with you, have gained popularity in recent years. While it is important to set boundaries in relationships, it's equally important to establish personal boundaries.

For instance, imagine you recently made some lifestyle changes like drinking less and exercising more, but your plans for a Saturday morning run got scrapped when you stayed out late and drank more than you planned to on Friday night.

If you stayed out and drank more than planned because you needed a night out, and chose to push your Saturday run to Sunday, then you prioritized your mental well-being. But, if you stayed out late and drank more than planned because your friends wanted you to, disregarding your Saturday morning plans, then you abandoned your personal boundaries.

When people abandon their personal boundaries, they often experience excessive thoughts and get trapped in feelings of guilt or shame. For example, someone compromising boundaries in a relationship, such as sending racy photos even when they do not want to will intensify emotional distress if the relationship ends.

Everyone has trouble sticking to their boundaries here and there. But if you notice you are disregarding your personal boundaries often, instead of being hard on yourself and replaying the past, your action is to focus on how you can create stronger boundaries in the future.

GRATITUDE

Another valuable way to create productive thoughts, and become your own hero, is through the practice of gratitude. When we embrace gratitude, we train our minds to notice and appreciate the positive aspects of life. This perspective shift helps us build the resiliency we need to get through difficult situations.

For example, instead of dwelling on a social slip at a party, you might feel grateful for stepping out of your comfort zone and socializing. Or you might view a work mistake as a chance to learn and grow instead of beating yourself up over it.

Practicing gratitude does not mean you won't feel any embarrassment or regret, or that you need to ignore your feelings. Instead, it helps you acknowledge and validate your emotions while maintaining a balanced perspective.

When practicing gratitude, it's important to avoid the trap of toxic positivity. Some people suggest you need to be grateful because others might want what you have e.g., "Someone would love the job you have." This is a toxic mindset that pressures you to feel grateful for things you're not genuinely thankful for. It will lead you to invalidate your feelings, making the emotions stronger and the situation worse.

Sure, someone might love the job you have, but someone else might hate it. How do we know these fictitious people have good judgment? It's human to want to grow and advance. Not liking your job could be a sign you're ready to move to a higher position, or it could indicate that your job is bad for your mental health. Genuine gratitude does not require you to invalidate your feelings.

Another misconception is that you need to be grateful at all times, leading to unnecessary pressure and unproductive thoughts. It's perfectly normal not to feel grateful 24/7. In fact, it would be weird if you did.

The great news is that when you're not feeling grateful, you can still get all the benefits of practicing gratitude by not forcing yourself to feel grateful for anything. You would say, "I'm grateful I'm not forcing myself to feel something I don't. I'm grateful I'm acknowledging my feelings. I'm grateful I'll get through this."

Embracing gratitude without invalidating your feelings is a powerful act of self-compassion that creates space to work through your emotions and feel better quicker. By practicing gratitude without invalidating your feelings, you reduce unproductive thoughts and will bounce forward after setbacks.

MY HERO

The most powerful force in this world is someone who has their own back. By becoming your own hero, you protect yourself completely, and relieving others of the burden to rescue you allows you to show up authentically in relationships. You will be less susceptible to manipulation and will not tolerate mistreatment. People will notice and feel at peace around you. They, too, will feel comfortable showing up as their authentic selves.

While the idea of saving yourself may seem daunting, and it might be upsetting to give up the idea that someone is going to come and rescue you, being your own hero is not an obligation; it's a privilege. You don't *have* to be your own hero, you get to be.

RULE #4: I CAN REJECT WHAT OTHERS THINK

While it may seem like common sense, this rule is easier said than done. Most of us tend to care too much about what other people think, leading us to prioritize their opinions over our own. While it's normal to seek approval, and want others to like us, relying too heavily on external opinions will lead to self-abandonment.

In reality, people's opinions are just their own subjective thoughts. How do we know their thoughts are productive? Why do their thoughts matter to us? And why should we give weight to opinions that may not contribute positively to our lives?

Instead of automatically accepting what people say or think, we need to focus on evaluating if their thoughts matter or if outside perspectives are actually helping us. Productive thinking involves prioritizing our opinion over others. By doing so, we empower ourselves to make decisions aligned with our values and goals.

ARE THEIR THOUGHTS PRODUCTIVE?

If someone criticizes your appearance, why should you care? They aren't giving any helpful advice. Are they the owner of a modeling agency? Do you need them to like the way you look so you can earn money so you can eat? Even if they are someone you like, nice people don't go around saying mean things like that. You're allowed to stop liking them.

While it's important to remain open to outside opinions and advice, your opinion of yourself is what matters most. And while outside opinions can help you gain different perspectives, other people's opinions typically don't really carry much weight.

People share their opinions freely and easily on a variety of topics, like your looks, how they think the world works, dating, fashion choices, or career advice. But not all feedback is beneficial, and not all advice is good advice.

Sometimes, even if they mean well, people can be negative because they're stuck in their own problems and unproductive thoughts. Remember, people can think whatever they want, but most people "overthink" (aka think unproductively).

Imagine someone attempts to do something and fails. Then they find out you're trying to do the same thing. Even if you're doing it differently, have different skills, and are doing it at a different time, they might try to discourage you.

They think that since they couldn't do it, no one can, but throughout history people have been doing things that others thought were impossible. It doesn't mean the naysayer is mean or a "hater;" they just have an unproductive mindset. Nonetheless, their limitations are not yours.

CHANGING THE SUBJECT

I developed a technique called "change the subject" to help me remember that people's opinions are their thoughts, not reality. It helps me not take things personally or give too much attention to other people's thoughts and involves reframing statements so they are about the person who made them.

So if someone says, "You are [insult]," you change it to, "You think I am [insult]?" This simple shift changes the focus and will stop you from internalizing negativity. This will help you quell unproductive thoughts and have others take responsibility for the things they say.

You may be surprised by how people respond when you remind them that their opinions are a reflection of themselves. But if they are really adamant, you have the right to ask for evidence to support their claims. Asking for proof challenges them to justify their viewpoint.

DIGGING DEEPER

While negative comments can sting, if a particular comment sticks with you, it's often a sign of a deeper insecurity. For instance, if someone commented on your looks while you were still growing into yourself, you may now have an insecurity about your appearance.

But instead of focusing on the people who make these comments, it's time to look inside. Beauty is different for everyone, and the ugly in this world is the pressure for us to abandon ourselves to fit into unrealistic beauty standards.

So if you can't stop thinking about someone who told you that you are going to fail, it might mean their negativity hurt, but it could also mean you need more confidence in what you are doing. When people first started criticizing my writing, saying no one would read it etc., it really stung, but I used those comments to realize how much I wanted to write. Then I used that feeling to fuel my personal growth. And hey, thanks for proving the naysayers wrong!

VISUALIZATION

To challenge the unhealthy idea that other people's opinions are more important than your own, you can use a powerful technique called visualization. Visualization is like a superpower, helping you reach your goals by imagining your desired outcomes. Here we'll use visualization to shift the perspective that what others say or think about you is more important than what you think about yourself.

Some people find it helpful to close their eyes and mentally visualize, others prefer writing it out, and some prefer a combination of both. Choose what works best for you. To get started, let's look at common scenarios where we are encouraged to prioritize other people's opinions over our own:

- People saying you need to look a certain way to be considered beautiful.
- Pressure to give up your dreams and focus on societal expectations.
- Parents or others pushing you to only pursue popular hobbies.
- Being told not to cry or show emotions because it's perceived as weak.
- Feeling obligated to conform to traditional gender roles.

To change this perspective, think about a time when someone made you feel like their opinion (or the opinion of other people) was more important than your happiness. Now, reimagine that same situation, but with that person cheering you on and telling you to put yourself first. Picture what this supportive environment looks like. What kind words do you hear? How does this new situation feel? How would your life be?

ELEVATOR PITCH

Another visualization technique to reduce the impact of negative comments, and to not give opinions so much weight, is the "elevator pitch." In business, an elevator pitch is a concise presentation, typically lasting thirty-seconds to one-minute, aimed at introducing yourself and your key points to potential investors. It is called an "elevator pitch" because that is roughly the time you would have if you were riding an elevator with a business investor at a conference.

My elevator pitch for The Thought Method Company would be "Hi, I'm Lyndsey, the creator of The Thought Method Company where we empower people by helping them take control of their thoughts and mental health."

To apply this technique, imagine the person who made a negative comment is the one giving you their pitch. (I have a lot of fun with these.)

> **THEM:** Hey, I'm an Internet Stranger. I am sad inside, and as the saying goes, "misery loves company," so I want to be mean and hurt others. I am going to insult you.
> **YOU:** Ah, OK. Thanks, but no thanks, Internet Stranger.

> **THEM:** Sup, I'm Random Dude. I have a hard time managing my emotions, so when you said no to the date, the rejection hurt my feelings. I threw a tantrum and called you an expletive.
> **YOU:** Ah, great, thanks, emotionally somewhat aware Random Dude?

In these scenarios, reframing the negative comments as an elevator pitch helps you detach yourself from hurtful words and maintain control over your emotional response. You'll reject the negativity and assert your boundaries effectively.

SOCIAL SCALING

Another effective technique for reducing the need for excessive external reassurance is to look at social situations on a scale. We are led to believe that most social situations are high stakes, believing they'll determine the course of our lives. For instance, we approach a first date as if it will either make or break our future, questioning, "What if they're 'The One'?" And we view every job interview as crucial, believing it will change our entire career trajectory. However, thinking this way only leads to pressure, excessive worrying, unproductive thoughts, and stress.

A first date isn't that crucial. Even if the person seems perfect on their dating profile, they might not be the right match for you, and that's okay. It's not personal; there are a lot of people in the world—not everyone will click with each other.

Imagine considering first dates as an exciting chance to meet someone new, rather than a potential life-changer. Instead of worrying about whether they like you or if the date will lead to something more, focus on getting to know a new person and learn about their interests. After the date, you can decide if you want to see them again. If they're interested, that's great! If they're not, it's better to know sooner rather than later.

Similarly, while job interviews can be stressful, especially if you've been searching for a job for a while or you really like the position, they need to be approached with a neutral view. Apart from what you've read in the job posting and online reviews about the company, you don't know much about the actual job or the company. The first interview is as much about you finding out if the position *suits you* as it is about them deciding if you're a good fit. You should, of course, prepare and do your best, but if you approach the interview as an opportunity for both you and the company, you will be better off than if you view it as a make-or-break scenario.

By reframing social situations in this manner, we realize that they are not as critical as we make them out to be. While a successful date or job interview *can* be life-changing, they do not define our entire existence. Ultimately, the most transformative change in our lives comes from focusing on ourselves and how we choose to show up in social situations.

PRIORITIZING PEACE

We don't often hear *how* to reject terrible advice and viewpoints. Instead, we're often reminded that people aren't paying as much attention to us as we think. Funny enough, this advice stems from the same issue of giving too much importance to other people's opinions. To think productively, it's crucial to prioritize your thoughts and feelings before considering other people's advice. Even if advice is well-intended, others may lack the skills or abilities you have; they might think something is impossible when it's actually achievable for you.

The most important thing to remember is that what you think of yourself, being your own hero, and focusing on your goals, are more important than what others think. While society often emphasizes the importance of relationships with others, *the most important relationship you'll ever have is with yourself.* We're conditioned to seek approval from others and hope that other people will like us, but do we like them? We're encouraged to make our parents proud, but are we proud of them? We're told to take advice, but is the advice helpful?

RULE #5: I ACCEPT WHAT I CANNOT CONTROL

Every day we are pressured to control parts of our lives that we can't. This pursuit is often fueled by the misconception that control equals power, leading us to chase after it, abandoning our values in the process. But true power comes from having a healthy relationship with control.

If your relationship with control is unhealthy, you will think you have more or less power over a situation than you really do. When faced with the inevitable, the things beyond your control, you may resort to repetitive thoughts in order to gain the illusion of power. While you can't change situations in real life, you can "control" it in your mind. This gets you stuck and in those annoying thought loops we keep talking about.

Improving your relationship with control is a valuable skill that will help you create productive thoughts. It helps you focus on the things you *can* control, like building better habits, being your own hero, improving social skills, and living in the moment.

CAN, CAN SOMEWHAT, CANNOT

Even though it's natural to want to control, it's important to recognize when you're trying to control the things that you can't. One way to do this is by categorizing aspects of your life into what you can fully control, what you can somewhat influence, and what is entirely beyond your control.[1]

Things within your control include the thoughts you focus on, your words, and your actions. You have the power to choose your mindset, express yourself authentically, and take intentional steps toward your goals. Things beyond your control include other people's opinions, their words, actions, and emotions. You cannot dictate how others perceive you or react to situations because everyone has their own perspectives and responses.

Then there are items that fall into the category of what you can *kind of* control. For example, you cannot guarantee an interview will go well, but you can try to influence a positive outcome by preparing and presenting yourself confidently. And while you cannot control how people perceive you, you can try to make good impressions by focusing on your communication style and appearance.

List as many things as you can think of for each category. I put a few examples in each group to help you get started:

CAN CONTROL	CAN SOMEWHAT CONTROL	CANNOT CONTROL
• What you focus on • How you act • What you say	• How well an interview goes • People's perceptions of you	• What other people think • What other people say or do • How other people feel

While we are taking a general view here, identifying what you can and cannot control is valuable for various life situations like dating, job interviews, and career changes. Some common situations that can lead to repetitive thoughts because of an unhealthy relationship with control include:

- Reflecting on past mistakes
- Disagreements and arguments
- Dating
- Planning trips
- Career changes

Accepting the limitations of your control may be challenging, but it is essential for creating resilience and emotional well-being. By acknowledging, and embracing, the aspects of life that are beyond your control, you create a sense of peace and empowerment, reducing the need for mental chatter.

ACCEPTANCE

After identifying what you can and can't control, it may be hard to accept the things beyond your control—especially if you've gone through trauma, someone you like doesn't feel the same way about you, or something you were excited about doesn't work out. This is when it's most helpful to accept things as they are.

Acceptance involves understanding and embracing the reality of a situation. Some people try to achieve acceptance by saying "everything happens for a reason," but that's not acceptance, it's unproductive, all-or-nothing thinking. This mentality might temporarily help you ignore your feelings, but will not help you in the long run. True acceptance is acknowledging the randomness of life without resistance. Sometimes, bad things happen to good people and good things happen to bad people.

Acceptance doesn't mean giving up or being passive. It is an empowered choice, a decision to understand the reality of a situation and react in a way that matches your values and goals. Here's an example of a non-acceptance versus acceptance response after not getting a promotion:

> **Not Accepting:** You continually dwell on not getting the promotion, feel mad, defeated, and consumed by negative thoughts about your worth and capabilities. You play the situation over and over in your mind leading to a downward spiral of unproductive thoughts.
>
> **Acceptance:** Acknowledging feelings of disappointment, you tell yourself you can't change what happened. You concentrate on being kind to yourself, taking time to figure out what you want to do next. You ask for advice and consider new opportunities that align with your goals.

Integrating acceptance into your mindset requires practice, especially in situations that caused a great impact, like making a big financial mistake or being a victim of abuse. In these situations, acceptance will still work, but it may take time as you sort through intense emotions and come to terms with what happened. To achieve acceptance, it is important to both validate your feelings and remind yourself:

- You can't change the past.
- You couldn't know what you didn't know.
- Bad things happen to good people.
- Sometimes we are in the wrong place at the wrong time.
- There is no excuse for abuse.

It is also helpful to remove reminders or to not focus on certain aspects of a situation. Like if you make a financial mistake, it is best not to continually check your bank statements until the feelings settle. If you were a victim of abuse, it would be helpful to focus on calming your nervous system and staying away from violent movies or true crime documentaries.

Creating a short phrase to repeat as a gentle reminder will help you get started. While I was working to accept the trauma in my life, I found the phrase "I am safe" helped me calm my thoughts and come to acceptance. By repeating "I am safe," I was able to bring myself to present awareness and accept that while the abuse happened, it was in the past and I am safe now.

To work on acceptance, borrow my affirmation, or choose one of the affirmations below to serve as a friendly reminder:

- I accept what I cannot change, and I change what I can.
- I honor my emotions, and I allow them to flow.
- I embrace the present moment, just as it is.
- I let go of needing things to be perfect and accept when they're not.
- I trust the process, even when it's challenging.
- I find power in letting go of what I can't control.
- I let go of what no longer serves me.
- I am strong and can get through tough times.
- I am at peace or can find peace with what is.
- I am ready for new beginnings.
- I release the past and welcome what's happening now with love.
- I surrender to the natural flow of life.
- I embrace change as an opportunity for growth.
- I am resilient, adaptable, and capable of handling life's challenges.
- I find peace in accepting things as they are.

HEALTHY CONTROL

We are continually pressured to control things we can't, like worrying about what people will think (e.g., "Don't guys like women with..." or "Don't women like men who..."). To rise above this, it's important to continually remind ourselves of what we can, can somewhat, and cannot control. The more we practice this mindset, the sooner it will turn into a subconscious habit.

As you continually reinforce this awareness, you may also need to remind others. This looks like letting a well-intentioned friend know that you cannot control what men or women want and that you are going to prioritize your own wants over external opinions. It can also look like reminding family that you cannot control what other people think, but you can control what you prioritize in your life.

In the Template section, you'll find space to reflect on specific situations where you've encountered challenges related to control and writing prompts to help you explore more productive thoughts.

RULE #6: I AM A WORK IN PROGRESS

In April 2022, Warren Buffet, who at the time of writing is the fifth richest person in the world,[1] shared valuable advice at the Berkshire Hathaway annual conference. While his guidance helped listeners learn the best investment to "beat inflation," it emphasizes a recurring theme he has shared throughout his career: investing in yourself.

Here are his exact words: "The best investment by far is anything that develops yourself, and it's not taxed at all... Whatever abilities you have can't be taken away from you. They can't actually be inflated away from you."[2]

You are investing in yourself right now by learning how to create productive thoughts. To stay on track, you need to confront and reject an underlying, unproductive belief that holds many people back, a belief you might not realize you have: perfection.

PERFECTION IS NOT A HUMAN TRAIT

Due to societal pressures and unrealistic expectations, most people feel they need to know all the answers and be perfect. This mindset not only makes it hard for them to admit to their mistakes, or acknowledge areas of improvement, it also leads them to reject their human-ness and the natural urge to want to learn and grow. As a result, they find themselves stuck in unproductive thought.

When we try to be perfect, not only do we deny ourselves the opportunity for growth, we abandon our power. And when we don't feel like we can learn from our mistakes, we internalize them and believe they define us. This leads to obsessively thinking about past mistakes, and a deep fear of making future mistakes. We get trapped in rumination and regret while watching our lives pass by.

The first step toward reclaiming personal power is acknowledging that making mistakes is not only accept-able, it is an essential part of growth. Perfection is an unattainable human trait. You can be kind, strong, and lots of other things, but you can never be perfect. No one is perfect, and the people who appear to have it all together, well, they are just better at pretending. By recog-nizing how liberating it is to not know all the answers, and the value in imperfection, you introduce authenticity and fulfillment into your life.

RESPONSIBILITY PIE

Life presents us with a wide range of responsibilities, ranging from mundane tasks, like taking out the trash, to navigating complex social situations. Sometimes responsibilities are straightforward, like being on cheese dip duty for the holiday party. Other times, like when we are in situations we never expected to be in, responsibilities are not so clear. Adding to the confusion are people who define themselves by their mistakes. They avoid taking ownership or will wrongly assign it to others, sometimes resulting in victim blaming.

When responsibilities are vague, and people refuse or try to pass off ownership, we may take on more responsibility than is rightfully ours. If you're someone who tends to "overthink," or finds it hard to shake off thoughts after a traumatic experience, chances are, you're in a cycle of assuming too much responsibility.

This burden can be overwhelming. Things can feel heavy, leaving you trapped in unproductive thoughts and feelings of regret and shame. To break the cycle, and create productive thoughts, it's crucial to only take ownership for the things you are truly responsible for.

Focusing on your role in a situation encourages you to think productively and focus on what you can control, providing clarity so you can take action. This approach also encourages self-compassion and leads you to ask the right questions, empowering positive change and relieving guilt and shame.

A technique for determining responsibility without taking on undue blame is the "responsibility pie." By visualizing each aspect of a situation, and assigning the appropriate responsibility, you gain insight into your role and create a healthier perspective.

Let's say you are stuck in a cycle of dead-end relationships. Common advice is to question why you are attracting toxic or emotionally unavailable people. It places all responsibility on you. With this approach, you get stuck wondering what *you* are doing to attract unavailable people, and you pressure yourself to attract emotionally available people instead—as if there is some perfect thing you need to say or do.

This can lead you to dress different, act different, *be* someone different. The entire time you are hyper-focused on toxic people instead of yourself, which is only going to create unproductive thoughts and take you off track. In this case, it's effective to look at the situation holistically and consider the parts that other people play.

When you do this activity, you can draw a circle and give each aspect of a situation a piece of "pie," or you can use visualization, or list the items out. Here's what a listed responsibility pie would look like:

- A lot of emotionally unavailable single people —THEM
- Emotionally unavailable people throw a wide net—THEM

- Not having strong boundaries and letting
  unavailable people in —YOU

You can't control (and are not responsible for) who is attracted to you, but you have power over who stays in your life. Setting boundaries and expressing your needs helps filter out emotionally unavailable people. By prioritizing your wants and needs, you are focused on building healthy perspectives, which will lead to healthy relationships.

Responsibility pies also offer valuable insights for those coping with trauma. There is no excuse for abuse. If you've experienced any form of abuse—physical, sexual, or emotional—it's not your fault and you have no claim to that pie. The abuser bears 100 percent of the responsibility.

In cases of unfortunate accidents, like you being behind the wheel during a car crash, consider other factors like weather conditions, a light being out, or distraction due to a loud noise. You are responsible for what you did *behind the wheel*, but there is no way for you to know what you didn't know and some things are beyond your control.

REFLECTION

Once you've outlined what you're responsible for, it's time to approach the past in a helpful way with reflection. Reflection, unlike rumination, is an intentional replaying of past situations with a goal—to focus on how you can improve. While this method often relies on reimagining events in your mind, if there's a really embarrassing memory that keeps bothering you, writing it down might be most helpful.

There are different ways to approach reflection. Here is a ridiculously effective three-step process. It can be used for a variety of situations, since most "overthinking" revolves around social interactions, we will use that as an example.

Imagine you keep thinking about something embarrassing you said at a social event.

> **STEP ONE:** Identify what you *could* and *couldn't* control in the situation. Remember, you have control over what you say, but you can't control how other people respond. Sometimes things we say are funny to some people but not to others.

> **STEP TWO:** Focus on actionable steps. Do you need to say sorry? Who would you apologize to? How should you apologize? If you're not sure, ask a friend if they think you offended anyone. For example, you could say, "Hey, I keep thinking about that silly thing I said at the party. Do you think I upset anyone? I didn't mean to."

> **STEP THREE:** The most important step. It involves imagining how you wish you had acted in

the past instead of dwelling on your actual behavior, and helps you understand *why you're bothered* by what happened, giving you space to create strategies to better handle a similar situation in the future.

MISTAKES ARE LESSONS

Not learning from your mistakes is the biggest mistake you can make. Mistakes are valuable lessons and sometimes we can get stuck thinking about past mistakes because there is a lesson for us to learn. If you find yourself stuck in unproductive thoughts about a mistake, ask yourself what you can learn from it and work on acceptance. Imagine how you wish you had acted, and take any actions to correct your mistakes so you can grow.

Sometimes, it's as simple as imagining being more confident and worrying less about how other people react. Other times, embarrassing moments can be so overwhelming, it's hard to move on no matter how we think about it. It's important to set boundaries and limit how much you think about the past. Try telling yourself, "I'll think about this embarrassing thing for thirty minutes, then I'll do something fun." When the thirty minutes are up, make a conscious effort to shift your focus from the situation. You can use techniques you learned in Rule #2: I Will Live in the Present to aid in the process.

By focusing on improvement, you reinforce the idea that personal growth is more valuable than striving for perfection. This mindset encourages you to continually invest in yourself, helps combat unproductive rumination and equips you to better manage similar situations in the future.

RULE #7: I TAKE ONE STEP AT A TIME

With two-day delivery and advertisements promising life transformations in minutes, instant gratification has become the norm. Social media adds to this effect by distorting our view of other people's accomplishments. While scrolling, we see the end result but not the effort or time it took for someone to achieve their success. This leads us to underestimate the time and dedication required for personal growth and goal achievement.

Expecting quick results is impractical and sets us up for failure. When we don't see quick results, it's common to look for shortcuts, which only leads to frustration and more failure. Personal growth, especially changing unproductive thoughts, is a gradual process that takes patience and persistence. While it's natural to want to stop repetitive thinking as quickly as possible, it's important not to rush the process.

To build productive thoughts, you need to challenge unrealistic expectations. Instead of stressing about how long it will take to achieve goals, focus on making steady progress one step at a time. By embracing this approach you'll make progress quicker.

LADDER TECHNIQUE

A method to develop skills and gain a well-rounded viewpoint is what I like to call the ladder technique. It involves breaking down large goals into smaller steps so you stay motivated and don't get overwhelmed. This keeps your focus on achieving the goal instead of getting caught in unproductive thoughts or trying to rush the process, and is particularly effective in personal development, where gradual progress is key.

If you attempt a running dash to the top of the ladder, you will likely fail. But if you work step by step, you could already be headed toward step two. It's basically the idea that slow and steady wins the race. For instance, if you want to improve your social skills, transforming from being the shy person in the corner to the life of the party overnight is too unrealistic.

Here, you would start by visualizing how you would like to present yourself at parties and what kind of presence you would like to have. You can also pinpoint what particular social interactions make you feel apprehensive and find small ways to incorporate them into your daily routine as a confidence-building exercise. This might involve consciously opting for interactions with cashiers instead of using self-checkout at a store, or simply making eye contact and exchanging greetings with people while walking down the street.

The ladder technique can also help with situations that trigger your unproductive thoughts. You may think you "overthink everything," but that's all-or-nothing thinking, and unproductive. It's helpful to take one step at a time by identifying which situations trigger unproductive thoughts the most. From there you can use the ICE Method to uncover and challenge what thoughts are leading you in a spiral. You can also recognize situations where you tend to think productively and use them as inspiration for creating productive thoughts.

Another important thing to consider is adding action to the thoughts. As the laws of physics have determined, an object in motion stays in motion. Sometimes taking that first step can be the most difficult. If you feel over-whelmed by the very idea of cleaning your house, start by putting things where they belong—dishes in the kitchen, clothes in the laundry basket. Sometimes all you need is less thinking and more action.

To write this book I didn't sit down and *boom* it was writ-ten. It took me a few years of writing articles and sharing my work in writers' groups and getting feedback. This work was published six years after I decided I would regret never fulfilling my dream of publishing a book. Some people might be thinking, *Six years?! OMG, that's a lot.* But if you look at life holistically, it's not. And I did more than write a book in those six years; I improved a lot of skills, and the confidence I gained along the way is invaluable. While taking years to accomplish something may sound long, if you don't start now, you will wish you did.

CELEBRATE SMALL WINS

Tracking progress for non-physical personal development goals can be challenging, there is no scale or measuring stick to use, but it is important for you to celebrate any success—no matter how seemingly small. For example, if you notice you are no longer thinking as much about something that used to trigger repetitive thoughts, that's a win! In fact, you making it this far in the book is a win! Come to think of it, you being at a level of self-awareness to recognize your unproductive thoughts is also a win!

While working to create productive thoughts, it's normal to experience ups and downs, and to feel disheartened at times. You may struggle to identify unhealthy thoughts in the moment, but noticing those thoughts afterward is still a step forward. Remember, awareness is the first step toward change.

Typically, we are harder on ourselves than others. Be kind to yourself during this process and celebrate small victories along the way. Take time to acknowledge your growth—sometimes it helps to imagine you are celebrating the success of a friend.

As you celebrate your own wins, you also need to stop laughing at other people's cringe. Unless they are laughing, too, do not make fun of or laugh at someone's embarrassing moments. Doing so reinforces negative thought patterns. You tell your brain that laughing at other people's embarrassments is normal, so you will assume everyone is laughing at yours too, even when they aren't.

NOT ALL STEPS ARE FORWARD

At some point we get tricked into thinking that growth happens in a straight line, and if we go back to old habits, all progress is lost. While we attempt new things, we may feel like we're failing if we slip or do not see a lot of progress up front. When really, us noticing we slipped is progress. So, while you may feel that you are taking two steps back, you probably already took five steps forward and just didn't realize it.

It's important to appreciate advances that make life easier, but we need to separate ourselves from them. Skills do not come in two-day delivery. Some skills may take a lifetime to master, and while that may sound daunting, it is very rewarding. Investing in yourself is the greatest investment you can make, and as you continue to build skills, you'll see a compounding return on your investment. Each skill makes it easier to build more, creating a cycle of growth and self-improvement.

CHECK-IN

Some authors say they sat down and wrote their book effortlessly. Good for them. For me, writing a book required hard work, grit, and a refusal to give up. There was a point where I almost did give up. As a first-time writer, I encountered a lot of challenges, and the editing process was overwhelming. I was proud of myself when I broke it down into small pieces, committing to edit two sections a day (the ladder technique).

By day two I was on a roll. Tempted to edit more than just two sections, I did not want to get burned out, so I stuck with my original goal (personal boundaries). Then, tragedy struck. I lost a week's worth of progress to what tech support called a "corrupted file." Not only was the work gone, I was being blamed for the file being corrupted, even though I saved everything like I was supposed to (responsibility pie).

Before I lost the edits I was in a state of flow. After a long writing process, I was finally seeing a glimmer, a light at the end of the tunnel so this was a particularly crushing setback. It felt like I could not succeed no matter what I did. Making the situation worse, I had to pay for tech support to help me even though it was their product that failed me. Then all I received was them finger-pointing at the computer company and the computer company pointing the finger back (cannot control).

I kept thinking about worst-case scenarios (catastrophizing), that the book will never be finished (all-or-nothing thinking) and that there was no point. While I could identify the unproductive thinking, and have the capacity to recognize more productive thoughts (ICE Method), my mind was rejecting them. Then I was plagued by the irony that I am teaching others to have productive thoughts, and here I was grappling with my own, unproductive thinking (perfectionism).

It got to a point where enough was enough and I needed to check in with myself, I needed to ask myself an important question: do you really want this? At first, I wasn't sure. So I then asked myself: what will you do instead then, what's next? And while I tried to find an answer, my thoughts finally calmed enough for me to feel. I realized I was so upset because this is really important to me. There was a real fear that I was going to start editing again, and then lose all of my edits, again. Kind of like people who, after a bad breakup, are nervous to get back in the dating pool and afraid of getting hurt again.

Even though it bothered me to no end that I was now a week past my original completion date, and that taking more time off would take me further away, I needed to tend to my emotions (acceptance). There was a lot of crying. I'm talkin, Kim Kardashian ugly crying. Then, after a week on the couch watching reruns of '90s sitcoms and cuddling with my cat (living in the meow), I knew I needed to get back (take action).

In the beginning it was difficult to come back to the document and redo the work that I lost. My intrusive thoughts kept telling me it was never going to be as good as the earlier version. I was nervous I was going to do a lot of work and a file would be corrupted again. Well-intentioned people told me to just take my time, but there is only so much time someone can take. I was in a rut and needed to get back out there (be my own hero). I am happy that I did and celebrated the win that, even though my emotions temporarily got the best of me, I was able to continue pursuing my goal.

I tell you this story to continue the message of taking it one step at a time, and that even though we do not see the failure and setbacks that go into other people's success, those failures and setbacks are there.

In the context of this book, we are at the conclusion, but in the grand scheme of things, this is the beginning of you taking control of your thoughts and your life. Your "overthinking" wasn't just annoying mental chatter, it was a sign you needed to come back to yourself, it was you identifying the thoughts that were leading you away from who you truly are. As someone who has been through the process, it is my honor to help you build a strong foundation and help you get started on the life-changing work ahead.

Keep in mind that being kind to yourself can be hard, especially in this world. Remember, you do not know what you do not know. You will be surprised, and likely confused and frustrated, at times. You might feel hopeless and need a break. Take the break, even if you do not want to, but make sure not to get stuck in the comfort of relaxation. If you ever feel stuck, refer to this book and use it as a guide. I hope just the sight of it will give you a friendly reminder that you are not alone. May it bring some laughter and lightness to what can otherwise be a very heavy process.

Reframing your thoughts can be tough. People say that challenges make us stronger, but most of us have already had more challenges than we would like, and we are stronger than we ever thought we would need to be. This can lead us to desire a quick fix, wishing we could flip a switch so we can turn off our thoughts. But the work of creating a more productive mindset will be one of the most rewarding things you will ever do.

While you might long for the end result, the process itself is the most fulfilling part. These are the "good ole days." This isn't just overcoming "overthinking;" this is you coming back to yourself. It can take years to overcome some stubborn thought habits, but the more you work at it the easier it becomes. Then, it will become second nature and you'll be happy you started when you did.

So hey, thanks for showing up for yourself; it's not an easy thing to do. Now go listen to "Holding Out for a Hero" by Bonnie Tyler, think about how you are your own hero, and dance around your house like everyone is watching but their opinions don't matter.

TEMPLATES

ICE METHOD

Situation Nickname: _____

Identify

Describe the situation. Write as much detail as you can. What are the unproductive or "overthinking" thoughts? Can you identify any cognitive distortions or thoughts that are coming from a fixed mindset or lack of confidence?

_____

_____

_____

_____

_____

_____

Challenge

Are you making assumptions? Do you have any facts to back up your thoughts? What are some productive thoughts you can have? What would you say to a friend if they were in the same situation?

_____

_____

_____

_____

_____

_____

Evaluate

How will productive thoughts help reduce your repetitive mental chatter? How good will it feel to have productive thoughts and stay aligned with your values and goals?

_____

_____

_____

_____

_____

NOTES:

ICE METHOD

Situation Nickname: _____

Identify
Describe the situation. Write as much detail as you can.
What are the unproductive or "overthinking" thoughts?
Can you identify any cognitive distortions or thoughts
that are coming from a fixed mindset or lack of
confidence?

_____

_____

_____

_____

_____

_____

Challenge
Are you making assumptions? Do you have any facts to
back up your thoughts? What are some productive
thoughts you can have? What would you say to a friend if
they were in the same situation?

_____

_____

_____

_____

_____

_____

Evaluate

How will productive thoughts help reduce your repetitive mental chatter? How good will it feel to have productive thoughts and stay aligned with your values and goals?

_____

_____

_____

_____

_____

_____

NOTES:

ICE METHOD

Situation Nickname: _____

Identify
Describe the situation. Write as much detail as you can.
What are the unproductive or "overthinking" thoughts?
Can you identify any cognitive distortions or thoughts
that are coming from a fixed mindset or lack of
confidence?

_____

_____

_____

_____

_____

_____

Challenge
Are you making assumptions? Do you have any facts to
back up your thoughts? What are some productive
thoughts you can have? What would you say to a friend if
they were in the same situation?

_____

_____

_____

_____

_____

_____

Evaluate

How will productive thoughts help reduce your repetitive
mental chatter? How good will it feel to have productive
thoughts and stay aligned with your values and goals?

_____

_____

_____

_____

_____

_____

NOTES:

CONTROL

Situation Nickname: _____

Identify
What were you trying to control that you can't?

_____

_____

_____

Challenge
What can you control?

_____

_____

_____

Evaluate
How satisfying will it feel to prioritize what you can control and accept what you can't? How will this help you achieve goals?

_____

_____

_____

_____

CAN CONTROL

CAN SOMEWHAT CONTROL

CANNOT CONTROL

NOTES:

CONTROL

Situation Nickname: _____

Identify
What were you trying to control that you can't?

_____

_____

_____

Challenge
What can you control?

_____

_____

_____

Evaluate
How satisfying will it feel to prioritize what you can control and accept what you can't? How will this help you achieve goals?

_____

_____

_____

_____

CAN CONTROL	CAN SOMEWHAT CONTROL	CANNOT CONTROL

NOTES:

CONTROL

Situation Nickname: _____

Identify
What were you trying to control that you can't?

_____

_____

_____

Challenge
What can you control?

_____

_____

_____

Evaluate
How satisfying will it feel to prioritize what you can control and accept what you can't? How will this help you achieve goals?

_____

_____

_____

_____

CAN CONTROL	CAN SOMEWHAT CONTROL	CANNOT CONTROL

NOTES:

NOTES

INTRODUCTION

1. Nolen-Hoeksema (2016), p. 38.
   Researcher Nolen-Hoeksema discusses the gender divide in "overthinking" in her book *Women Who Think Too Much*; however, based on my research, I disagree with this notion and believe that overthinking is not gender-specific.
2. Kaiser, B. N., Haroz, E. E., Kohrt, B. A., Bolton, P. A., Bass, J. K., & Hinton, D. E. (2015). Thinking too much: A systematic review of a common idiom of distress. *Social Science & Medicine, 147*, 170–183. https://doi.org/10.1016/j.socscimed.2015.10.044
   Several sources explore the connection between "overthinking" and mental health disorders. I specifically selected this article because I appreciate the authors' emphasis on building community and reducing stigma surrounding mental illness.
3. Irvine (2009), pp. 85-101.
4. Herman (2015), p. 25.
5. Jung (1968), p. 5.
6. Herman (2015), p. 133.

VALUE SETTING

1. Cohen (2022), p. 136.

THOUGHT BASICS

1. Encyclopedia Britannica. (2023, September 19). *Information theory. Encyclopedia Britannica.* https://www.britannica.com/science/information-theory/Physiology
   Multiple resources provide varying numbers, but I rely on this article because it aligns with other sources I've found.
2. Encyclopedia Britannica. (2023, September 19). *Information theory. Encyclopedia Britannica.* https://www.britannica.com/science/information-theory/Physiology

3. Greenberger & Padesky (2015), pp. 152-153.

FIXED MINDSET

1. Dweck (2006), Introduction.

UNHELPFUL THINKING HABITS

1. Burns (2006), p. 10.
2. Burns (2006), p. 16.
3. Greenberger & Padesky (2015), p. 95.

THE CHANGE PROCESS

1. Greenberger & Padesky (2015), p. 63.

RULE #1: I AM THE OBSERVER

1. Wilson, T. D., Reinhard, D. A., Westgate, E. C., Gilbert, D. T., Ellerbeck, N., Hahn, C., Brown, C. L., & Shaked, A. (2014). Just think: The challenges of the disengaged mind. *Science, 345*(6192), 75–77. https://doi.org/10.1126/science.1250830
2. Tolle (2008), pp. 54-55.

RULE #2: I LIVE IN THE PRESENT

1. Tolle (1997), pp. 33-36.

RULE #5: I ACCEPT WHAT I CANNOT CONTROL

1. Irvine (2009), p. 89.

RULE #6: I AM A WORK IN PROGRESS

1. Forbes. (n.d.). *The world's real-time billionaires*. Retrieved

December 22, 2023, from https://www.forbes.com/real-time-billionaires/

2. Csiszar, J. (2023, December 22). *Warren Buffett says the most critical investment lies within ourselves.* GOBankingRates. https://www.gobankingrates.com/investing/strategy/warren-buffett-says-the-most-critical-investment-lies-within-ourselves/

REFERENCES AND FURTHER READING

To keep it conversational, I kept citations to a minimum and focused on a select few texts that cover a broad range of information. This approach allows you to explore topics in depth without needing to purchase numerous additional books. In the "Notes" section, you will find the online works that were cited. If you're interested in learning more, the books that were referenced, along with recommended readings, are provided below.

CONFIDENCE, COMMUNICATION, AND SOCIAL SKILLS

Cohen, G. L. (2022). *Belonging: The science of creating connection and bridging divides.* W. W. Norton & Company.

Patterson, K., Grenny, J., McMillan, R., & Switzler, A. (2011). *Crucial conversations: Tools for talking when stakes are high* (2nd ed.). McGraw-Hill.

Voss, C., & Raz, T. (2016). *Never split the difference: Negotiating as if your life depended on it.* Random House.

CONTROL

Beattie, M. (2009). *Codependent no more: How to stop controlling others and start caring for yourself.* Simon & Schuster.

Irvine, W. B. (2009). *A guide to the good life: The ancient art of stoic joy.* Oxford University Press.

Neuharth, D. (2009). *If you had controlling parents: How to make peace with your past and take your place in the world.* HarperCollins.

CONSCIOUSNESS AND PRESENT AWARENESS

Jung, C. G. (Ed.). (1968). *Man and his symbols*. Dell Publishing.

Murphy, J. (2011). *The power of your subconscious mind*. Martine Publishing.

Sartre, J. P. (1992). *Being and nothingness*. Simon & Schuster.

Tolle, E. (2008). *A new earth: Awakening to your life's purpose*. Christian Publishing House.

Tolle, E. (1997). *The power of now: A guide to spiritual enlightenment*. Namaste Publishing.

MINDSET

Dweck, C. S. (2006). *Mindset: The new psychology of success*. Random House.

Kahneman, D. (2011). *Thinking, fast and slow*. Farrar, Straus and Giroux.

THOUGHTS AND THERAPY

Greenberger, D., & Padesky, C. A. (2015). *Mind over mood: Change how you feel by changing the way you think* (2nd ed.). Guilford Publications.

Burns, D. D. (2006). *When panic attacks: The new, drug-free anxiety therapy that can change your life*. Harmony.

McKay, M., Wood, J. C., & Brantley, J. (2019). *The dialectical behavior therapy skills workbook: Practical DBT exercises for learning mindfulness, interpersonal effectiveness, emotion regulation, and distress tolerance*. New Harbinger Publications.

Nolen-Hoeksema, S. (2016). *Women who think too much: How to break free of overthinking and reclaim your life*. Holt Paperbacks.

TRAUMA

Bancroft, L. (2003). *Why does he do that? Inside the minds of angry and controlling men*. Penguin.

Herman, J. L. (2015). *Trauma and recovery: The aftermath of violence – from domestic abuse to political terror*. Hachette UK.

Miller, A. (1997). *The drama of the gifted child: The search for the true self* (R. Ward, Trans., 3rd ed.). Basic Books.

AUTHOR'S NOTE

Every Wednesday, a group of entrepreneurs meet on Zoom. One entrepreneur presents their idea and the others give feedback. In October 2020, it was my turn. I was pitching a book series called Thoughtbooks, designed to help readers achieve specific goals by improving their thoughts.

Unlike other meetings, the feedback for Thoughtbooks was intense. Some people assumed I was trying to play doctor and that the whole concept would fail. The discussion got so heated moderators ended the meeting early.

Unfortunately, encountering negativity while sharing my passion for teaching others how to improve their thoughts is not new for me. A negativity that reflects the widespread mistrust in today's self-help industry.

Nowadays, it can feel like everyone is a so-called "expert." Who can you really trust? Adding fuel to the fire is the fact that most people face failure or setbacks when attempting personal development efforts. In fact, self-help and personal development burnout is leading people back to bad habits. We all know someone who has a drinking problem, or uses other forms of escape and negative coping, like excessive spending, binge-watching, or joking about being emotionally dead.

But behind these coping mechanisms is a lost and lonely person who desperately wants to feel and do better. Someone who does not know where to begin. Believe me, I know. I've been there. And I tried what they tell us to try, and those efforts failed me just like they fail everyone else.

Instead of believing the narrative that I was broken, I took a closer look and started seeing the flaws in conventional methods. I started learning, and saw firsthand that knowledge truly is power. Applying that knowledge transformed my life significantly.

The critics in that awful Zoom meeting were kind of right —I am not a doctor. But, unlike what they suggested, I am not trying to play one. I am someone who was fed up and refused to give up. Someone who created her own methods after a decade of research, study, and self-experimentation. Someone who changed her life by taking on new perspectives and improving the quality of her thoughts. Now, I want to share what I learned to help others, including you.

Though not meant to replace therapeutic or medical advice, here you will find what I wish I had when I was starting out—practical tools and curated knowledge to help you learn how to control your thoughts.

Overthinking, an issue that affects most people, was the obvious topic for the first Thoughtbook. Overthinking used to control my life, and like many others, it was a sign of larger mental health issues. But there is hope. Not only am I here with welcome information, I am proof that these methods work. Think about it—I am an ex-over-thinker who wrote a book about overthinking without overthinking it. OK, well, there was *a lot* of thinking involved, but it was intentional.

Working to improve yourself takes a lot of courage. The strength in me sees the strength in you.

Love, Lyndsey

ACKNOWLEDGEMENTS

Thank you to the overthinkers who responded to surveys and everyone who contributed to this book, including editors, designers, alpha and beta readers and writers' groups.

To my friends for listening to me vent my frustrations and struggles.

Thank you to the people who shared their stories of struggle with their mental health. At times I wondered if something like this was needed; you gave me the gentle reminder to keep going.

Thank you to Dr. Aaron T. Beck for his pioneering work in psychology and to mental health professionals—especially Dr. JB.

To Melody Beattie and authors who set out to help others develop, paving the path so people like me could do the same.

And thank you to Lundy Bancroft for letting me know "why he did that," giving me the courage to find my voice and help others find theirs.

Overthink

Lyndsey Getty

Thoughts
Are
Better
Shared

A Book Club Guide

a letter to readers

Hey there!

One of my favorite parts of writing *Overthink* was coming up with the examples. Many of them are drawn from my own life and the lives of my friends. In fact, Marcus's mishap was inspired by the time when my friend accidentally said "you too" to a waiter and then called me laughing, saying, "Why was he so hot?!"

I wanted to make sure the examples in the book covered different areas of life, so no matter what, you could find yourself in these pages. I hope some of the stories resonated with you and maybe even made you laugh.

Thank you for reading, and I hope you enjoy discussing your favorite parts of the book!

- Lyndsey

discussion guidelines

These guidelines create a foundation for healthy and thoughtful discussions, while ensuring participants feel supported and respected.

1. **Confidentiality is Key.** What's said in the discussion stays in the discussion. This creates a safe space for all participants to share their thoughts and feelings openly without fear of judgment or gossip.
2. **Respect All Perspectives.** Everyone has different experiences and viewpoints. Listen actively and respectfully, even if you don't agree. Avoid interrupting and make space for others to speak.
3. **No Fixing or Advising.** Unless someone asks for advice, avoid jumping in with solutions. The goal is to share and listen, not to solve or "fix" each other's problems.
4. **Mental Health Awareness.** If someone expresses distress or seems in need of help, gently encourage them to reach out to their therapist or call a mental health hotline (such as the **Suicide & Crisis Lifeline: 988**). The book club is a space for discussion, not professional mental health support.
5. **Nonjudgmental Space.** Avoid judgmental language and tone. This includes refraining from criticizing others' thoughts, opinions, or personal experiences.

6. **Participation Is Encouraged, but Optional.** While everyone is encouraged to participate, it's okay if someone wants to pass on a question or doesn't feel ready to share. Participation should be voluntary and without pressure.

7. **Keep it Constructive.** Constructive discussions help us grow, while negativity can hinder open communication. Focus on productive, thoughtful sharing and be mindful of how your words impact others

———

Constructive feedback offers thoughtful and respectful responses creating a supportive environment for discussion. It looks like:

- **Acknowledging contributions:** "I really appreciated your interpretation of that chapter. It made me think differently about the concept."
- **Offering friendly suggestions:** "Could the theme you mentioned be expanded by considering other viewpoints?"
- **Encouraging dialogue:** "What you said was interesting! I'd love to hear more about how you think that connects other areas in the book."

discussion questions

1. What do you think about the idea that "overthinking" is just unproductive thoughts? Did that perspective make you feel more empowered?
2. How often do you overthink? After taking the self-assessment, did you realize you overthink more than you initially thought?
3. What types of situations tend to trigger unproductive thoughts for you? Which "root cause" resonated with you the most?
4. What did you know about thoughts and thought processes before reading *Overthink*?
5. When reading about Marcus's mishap, did his story resonate with you? Why or why not?
6. Reflect on the change process. Were you surprised by your ability to change and manage your thoughts? How can you practice creating productive thoughts in your daily life?
7. What do you think will be your biggest challenge in creating productive thoughts?
8. What specific strategies or exercises from the book did you find most helpful? How can you incorporate them into your daily routine?
9. How can being your own hero benefit you in both personal and professional settings?
10. How do you think focusing on what you can, cannot, and can somewhat control will improve your daily interactions and relationships?

11. Were there any key moments or concepts that resonated with you? If so, what were they?

RESOURCES

The information and advice in this book are not a substitute for therapeutic or medical care. Please seek professional help if you believe you may have a condition. If you or someone you care about needs support or someone to talk to, here are two key resources that can help:

Suicide & Crisis Lifeline
A free, confidential 24/7 hotline for anyone in crisis or emotional distress.
988
988lifeline.org

The National Domestic Violence Hotline
A free, confidential 24/7 hotline for anyone experiencing domestic violence or questioning their relationship.
1-800-799-SAFE (7233)
thehotline.org

ABOUT THE AUTHOR

PHOTO BY: Zave Smith

Lyndsey Getty is the creator of Thought Intelligence and founder of The Thought Method Company. She lives in Philadelphia, Pennsylvania.

thoughtmethod.com
@thoughtmethod:

FEEDBACK IS A GIFT

Write to Us!
I'd love to hear about your experience with the book and how it has helped you (or how you think we can improve). Email me at lyndsey@thoughtmethod.com.

Your Review Matters!
Please help others discover *Overthink* by leaving a review on Amazon—it not only helps new readers but also supports indie authors like me.

For more books and updates:
thoughtmethod.com

The Thoughtbook Series

Overthink

calm thoughts

Stop overthinking and boost confidence.
Build adaptal thought patterns.
Control your thoughts.

lyndsey getty

Middle Think

balanced thoughts

Stop all-or-nothing thinking.
Build a balanced mindset.
Overcome perfectionism.

lyndsey getty

Clear Think

clear thoughts

Stop emotions from clouding your judgement.
Stay levelheaded under pressure.
Make smarter decisions.

lyndsey getty

Big Think

empowered thoughts

Remove mental blockers.
Grow and unlock your potential.
Build confidence and step into your power.

lyndsey getty

Middle Think: BalancedThoughts

balanced
thoughts

Stop all or nothing thinking.
Build a balanced mindset.
Overcome perfectionism.

lyndsey getty

DOES YOUR MIND JUMP BETWEEN EXTREMES, PERFECTIONISM, ALL-OR-NOTHING THINKING, FEELING LIKE THINGS WON'T GET BETTER?

Middle Think offers a powerful yet simple approach to breaking free from these mental traps. Instead of getting stuck in rigid thought patterns, you will learn how to embrace a balanced mindset that fosters clarity, confidence, and resilience.

With relatable examples and actionable strategies, this practical guide helps you shift from extreme thinking to a more flexible, realistic perspective. Key takeaways, include:

- How extreme thinking affects emotions, decisions, and relationships
- Practical techniques to recognize and reframe unhelpful thoughts
- Simple exercises to build mental balance and reduce stress
- Strategies to strengthen resilience and improve self-awareness
- Tools to navigate life's complexities with a clearer, steadier mindset

This is not about suppressing your thoughts, it is about transforming them. *Middle Think* gives you the tools to move beyond extremes and build a mindset that works for you, not against you.

Clear Think: Clear Thoughts

DO YOUR EMOTIONS CLOUD YOUR JUDGMENT? STRUGGLING TO STAY LEVELHEADED UNDER PRESSURE?

Clear Think offers a practical, no-nonsense approach to making better decisions, staying in control of your emotions, and thinking with confidence. Instead of letting stress and overthinking take over, you'll learn how to manage your mindset and stay clearheaded—even in high-pressure situations. With actionable strategies and relatable examples, this guide will help you:

- Separate facts from feelings to make sound decisions
- Strengthen emotional intelligence and improve self-awareness
- Build confidence by defining your boundaries and values
- Learn to respond thoughtfully instead of reacting impulsively
- Turn past mistakes into valuable opportunities for growth

You don't have to be ruled by emotions or stuck in reactive thinking. *Clear Think* gives you the tools to stay calm, focused, and in control no matter what life throws your way.

Big Think: Empowered Thoughts

Big Think

empowered
thoughts

Remove mental blockers.
Grow and unlock your potential.
Build confidence and step into your power.

lyndsey getly

ARE YOUR BELIEFS LIMITING YOUR POTENTIAL? DO MENTAL BLOCKERS AND THOUGHT HABITS HOLD YOU BACK?

Big Think reveals how deeply ingrained beliefs shape your choices, limit your growth, and keep you stuck in old patterns. Through a simple three-step process, this book helps you break free by identifying, challenging, and replacing mental blockers with empowering new perspectives. With real-world examples and practical advice, you'll uncover the beliefs holding you back, build confidence in your decisions, and create new opportunities for growth. Along the way, you'll learn how to:

- Find your voice and advocate for your needs
- Ditch external expectations and follow your true passions
- Embrace who you are and look inward for validation
- Turn struggles into opportunities
- Release shame and feel more connected
-

Packed with actionable strategies and relatable insights, *Big Think* helps you break past limitations and step into your full potential. It's time to rewire your mindset and take control of your future.

www.ingramcontent.com/pod-product-compliance
Lightning Source LLC
Chambersburg PA
CBHW060929120626
46557CB00003B/930

* 9 7 9 8 9 9 0 0 2 6 6 3 6 *